CW01560476

The Angel Within

Claire Robertson PhD

authorHOUSE®

AuthorHouse™ UK Ltd.
500 Avebury Boulevard
Central Milton Keynes, MK9 2BE
www.authorhouse.co.uk
Phone: 08001974150

First published by AuthorHouse 11/24/2009

ISBN: 978-1-4490-1413-1 (sc)

This book is printed on acid-free paper.

Dedications:

I wish to send a huge bouquet of love and gratitude to my Mum and Dad, who have been the Earth Angels who have given me the wings to fly, when I found it difficult to walk.

My brother, Simon, who has been an inspirational light in the dark.

My beautiful furry Angels Jupiter, Oberon, and Perseus who have followed me wherever my life lead.

And lastly to my Angels who have never allowed me to hide or get lost along the way.

Life flows in peaks and troughs, as all energy does and I was at one of life's troughs when I started to write this book. No matter what I did it didn't turn out the way I planned. I constantly asked my Angels for advice, but in my opinion they seemed determined not to hear it. Then one day while pondering my problems I started to receive what I considered to be some very strange advice from my Angels. I was sitting relaxing before starting a late shift at work and my eye was drawn to my two budgies. One is a very vibrant blue colour (called Pixie) and the other is a very pale golden colour (called Dixie). Dixie was preening her wing feathers and very clearly I heard a voice in my head saying "When was the last time you cleaned your wings". At the time I thought to myself – how very odd – but didn't ponder on it too much. Several weeks passed by and I was still in what I call limbo, that place where we tread time but achieve nothing. Then I was sitting in a training seminar at work when the same voice spoke again, and this time it kept saying "the Angel within, the Angel within". I had no idea what this meant. I had received previous guidance to write a book, and started to write a Faery novel introducing children and adults to the wonderful world of the Fae. An Angel book never occurred to me, as I felt there were many wonderful resources out there for people to draw on. Little was I to know what my Angels had planned for me….

Angels among us

The word Angel, is derived from the Latin word *Angelus* and the Greek work *angellos* which both mean "messenger". When I first started to work with Angels fulltime I always had my ego standing very firmly on one side asking me "who are you to be good enough to be communicating with these divine beings". While on the other side my Angels argued "who are you not to be". We are all divine sparks of light, whether we are still within the Angelic realms or whether we have chosen to incarnate into a human body for a brief time – we are all still children and student's to the divine.

There are many people in this world who perform minor miracles every day – who are beacons of light to everyone they meet. These are Angels who have incarnated into human form to help bring us closer to God and aid us in remembering our divine missions. Why would an Angel want to incarnate is the first question that sprung to my mind when I became aware of these wonderful beings. Why put yourself through so much pain and suffering when you can quite easily stay there in the Angelic realms where there is no pain, suffering, poverty, species extinction, and mistrust? This is a question that every incarnated Angel will have asked themselves at some point in their lives, and life is the answer. It is through experiencing the entire rainbow of emotions including the good and the bad that we can understand how others think and feel.

The second question that came to me was – What is an Incarnated Angel? I was shown that there are two instances that Angels take on a physical form in this world – the first to save someone if it is not their time to pass on, and the second when an Angel elects to take on a human life to intervene in a family which desperately needs help – and who cannot hear the answer any other way. They then get caught in the ego trap and reincarnation cycle.

Every one of us has a soul inside us, a beautiful divine spark of light that shines and helps illuminate situations to us when the darkness closes in around us – this is our Angel within. It is the voice that is steady when we are not, it is the feeling of calmness that comes over us when we take that deep breath that allows our creative energy to flow, and it is our connection to God and in turn our Angel and God's connection with each and every one of us.

Through performing personal readings and taking Angel Workshops, I have found that I belong to the group known as Incarnated Angels and I have recently noticed that it is this group of humans who are currently experiencing the most difficulties in life, and who are in desperate need of help in their own lives as they have disconnected from their "Angel within". I hope that through reading the following chapters that each one of these Angels can learn how to open their wings, clean them, and eventually learn to fly. Happy reading, my Angels, and may you fly so high you learn to sing with the Angels.

What is an Angel?

Throughout the history of mankind, there have always been beautiful, peaceful beings who have helped different cultures and were involved in the belief systems of those cultures. There are around 600 references to Angels in the Bible alone, and they also feature in the Talmud and the Koran. Angels are divine messengers, created by God, who act as a rainbow bridge between heaven and earth. They serve as a channel between the Creator to the created and back again, akin to a heavenly postal service. They are precious guides and guardians who stay by our sides helping us throughout our life here on earth. There are as many Angels as there are thoughts of love from God – too many to count. They are as stars in the night sky – countless and beautiful; watching us from the heavens.

Then I looked and heard the voice of many angels,
numbering thousands upon thousands, and ten
thousand times ten thousand.
They encircled the throne and the living creatures and
the elders.
-Revelations 5:11

They do not possess a physical body, and therefore do not live in the same energy plane as ourselves. They are often seen as "Angel lights" from the corner (or periphery) of our eyes – beautiful white sparkling lights made as Angels travel through time and space. Many people have asked me if Angels have wings? The answer is simple. I have seen Angels both with and without wings. They show themselves with wings so that we can identify them as Angels. They do not need wings to fly as they move instantaneously to where they need to be. Angels are beautiful beings of light, and have often been seen as pillars of light, twinkling lights, a white mist, or human shaped. They are beautiful, pure, tall beings which emanate light and feelings of peace and love.

Angels work as an emotional support system to their charges and aid in their emotional healing. Many physical ailments that my clients come to me with have an emotional cause, and therefore working with Angels can start the healing process from within. Your Angels have witnessed your good deeds, as well as your bad and still love you unconditionally. This is because Angels have no ego and therefore do not judge your actions; they merely love you and give you the strength and courage to continue.

By inviting your Guardian Angels into our lives we allow ourselves to reconcile heaven and earth within ourselves. There is no task that Angels cannot help with, in fact they are totally dedicated in helping you evolve spiritually as well as helping you in practical ways. All we need to do is find belief in ourselves and the faith to listen.

How do I know if I'm an Incarnated Angel?

Incarnated Angels are shy beings – like their Guardian Angel counterparts. We like to stay in the background and allow others to take the praise. We tend to make rules and expect ourselves and others to stick to them; there is also the little habit of not breaking rules and beings painfully honest to everyone. So the best advice is not to ask an Incarnated Angel friend what she thinks of your new hair style if you fear the worst!

We give our hearts away too easily as we believe the best in people, and are disappointed when we see the worst in people. An Incarnated Angel (through no choice of their own may I add) has a tendency to put a layer of extra weight around their middle to cushion their solar plexus area from excessive negative energy that they encounter.

When I look back at all the Incarnated Angels that I have worked with and encountered on my Angelic pathway, I have noticed that many of them tell very little about their real self. They hide themselves behind listening to others problems (and helping solve them), being life-coaches to their families and those they meet, and suffer general ill-health themselves.

One of my favourite quotes is by GK Chesterton. "Angels can fly because they take themselves lightly."

My wish for all the Incarnated Angels out there is to take yourself lightly. We have a tendency to take everything personally. A colleague or friend may say something to an Incarnated Angel – a throwaway comment – that will never again enter the person's head. However, by the time the average Incarnated Angel has gotten home the small molehill of a comment will have turned into a huge un-climbable mountain. Each of us has done it at some point in our lives – it wasn't just WHAT they said, but HOW they said it, WHY they said it, and what we interpret they meant by it. In other words we over-analyse situations, even many years later we are coming up with answers we should have said, and actions we should have taken.

I know that to other people this may sound strange, but this is the workings of an Incarnated Angel's mind, and to know them is to love them – wings and all.

It has been my experience that if you THINK you are an Incarnated Angel, you generally ARE. From an early age, Incarnated Angels will have loved Angel art, Angel ornaments, and crystals of all sorts and descriptions. Never would it have entered the mind of an Incarnated Angel NOT to believe in Angels, and working with Angels is as natural as singing our favourite song. Over the course of taking many workshops and classes I have noticed when introducing people to different energies – from Angels, to Faeries, to Ascended Masters and Goddesses, to Archangels – the people who connect continuously with the Angelic realms and receive clear, concise, and accurate information from the Angels are those who are themselves Incarnated Angels. It is natural to us, because that is where our souls have spent the most time – it is where we will once again return to when we have emerged from the re-incarnation loop, back to working with the heavenly realms.

Working with Angels is the greatest pleasure in my life – they are among my best friends and loyal guides. If I am a pebble that has been thrown into the lake of life, then my Angels are my closest ripples. There is nothing we cannot ask our Angels to help us with from the parking Angels to the cooking Angels to the revision Angels to the romance Angels to the parenting Angels all the way through to the Angels we use in everything we undertake. There is nothing we cannot ask them to help us with, and that is why Angels are the most valued and fabulous of all our guides. I would never think of leaving home without asking the four major Archangels to protect my car and having my guardian Angels inside with me. Throughout this book you will find me telling you parts of my story and why it is so important to WORK with our Angelic friends. They are there to make our lives easier in every way. I always ask and they always send me what is the most benevolent outcome for what I am working on. Whenever I look back on my life I can say without a doubt that I may not always get what I want but the

Angels always give me what I need......when you think about it, it is a safe place to be - **in the hands of God and the Angels**.

Learning how to connect to the Angel within

I feel this is the most important step in each person's journey into the world of working with Angels. Everyone can work with Angels in their own way, even though Incarnated Angels find this easier than those souls who derive from other realms. I have found that the first step to this is aligning yourself to the energy of your Guardian Angel (the most loyal and trusted friend that God has given your soul to guide and guard you). Every person in this world has at least two Guardian Angels, although Incarnated Angels seem to quite naturally attract more Angels into their lives and their everyday chores.

> For it is written, He shall give His Angels
> charge over thee, to keep thee.
> - Luke 4:10

Each of us has a Soul Guardian Angel who has been with us from the moment our soul was made many lifetimes ago and a Life-Purpose Guardian Angel to ensure that we reach our highest potential as we journey through this lifetime. They are with you every moment of every

10

day guiding you so that your life will run smoothly, and also so that you will have an insight into the situations you find yourself in.

I am very fortunate that I have the gift of being able to visualise Angels when I am working with them. I have tuned out seeing Angels and spirits all the time as it got very confusing who I was talking to on a daily basis! In my experience I have always seen Angels standing behind people, and in most people I have noticed them to be of a female and a male energy – a balancing of Yin and Yang – to give the guidance they give a balanced outlook. The female energy is a receiving energy, and the male energy is giving. I always encourage those who I teach to balance their energies so that their giving and receiving is in balance, and thus in balance with their Guardian Angels energies. It is also the best position for them to be in to whisper guidance into our ears!

Another position I have seen people's Guardian Angels in is what I refer to as the "protective" position, where the person has felt threatened or afraid and their Angels have positioned themselves to stand one in front of them, and one behind them, to block negative energy from reaching them.

All of my life I have felt slightly different to the people around me. I was very happy as a child to play on my own – I felt protected and loved. In saying that I was also happy to play with my brother and other children – I didn't exclude myself from the crowd, but neither did I have to be in a crowd to be happy. I was always happy in my own skin, knowing that I was loved and wanted by my parents. I feel that it was because I was in this loving environment that seeing and working with the Angels came very easily to me. As we give out love, it comes back to us again in all aspects of our life. In the beginning I could feel emotions around people – I could pick up atmospheres in a house and around people. As my gifts developed and I started to work with Angels they told me that to work as a fully functioning spiritual being then I had to see and accept the divinity in myself, so that I could see the divinity in others too. It would be through this loving gift that I would be able to work completely with the Angels without my human ego interfering - that is why the information I receive is so pure and filled with unconditional love for my clients. This divinity is what the Angels have told me is called the "Angel Within".

Meditation is the most important tool we have on our spiritual tool-belt and it is through this dedicated time working on ourselves that we begin to align ourselves with Angelic energies, and start our journey on the pathway to the Angelic Realms. Most people reading this will think to themselves "I haven't the time to fit meditation into my schedule". I can fully understand this in the rush of everyday life. So I ask you to try any of the following simple exercises on Angelic alignment throughout this book once a day. As you find time to fit one in, you will find that your Angels will start to find opportunities for you to fit others in. Once you have found that you have mastered the art of meditation you can progress further in your relationship with your Guardian Angels and ultimately with the Angel within.

Many of the people who attend my classes ask me the name of their Guardian Angels. My answer is always the same – ask your Angels! The name of the Guardian Angels that work with you in your life is personal, and finding their name is a personal quest. Even though I know the names of the Angels that I work with, I still call them Angels. Always remember that energy follows intent. Below is a gentle exercise that will allow you to find the names of your Guardian Angels:

Give yourself some time in nature and find somewhere to sit and rest for a while. As you are sitting listening to nature allow yourself to absorb the energy and peace that surrounds you. Listen to the language of the birds that sing around you, as it is my belief that their song is on the low vibrational end of the Angelic choirs. As you find yourself drawn into this sound of divine magic gently ask your Guardian Angels their names. Allow whatever word, name, or emotion that comes to you. This is the name that they wish you to use at this time. Always check in regularly with your Angels as I have found that although the Angel is the same, sometimes the name changes to aid you with the situation you are working with in your life.

Who am I to work with Angels?

Someone once asked me why would beings so beautiful and holy as the Angels want to work with us here on earth? Surely there is inherent badness in all of us, therefore why would they want to work with us?

I decided to ask my Angel friends about this, and when I meditated upon this my Angels showed me a night sky so clear and dark with beautiful stars throughout it. As I continued to view this scene the stars started to move around the dark sky and every so often collide with each other. My scientific mind told me that there should have been a marvellous explosion at the collision of these two stars but a beautiful coloured Aura surrounded them when they did and I had a feeling of such peace that it took my breath away.

I asked my Angels to explain what I had witnessed in my meditation vision and they told me their wonderful version of beings of light. Every one of us is a beautiful spark of divine holiness. When we incarnate we do not remember previous lifetimes, we do not remember our life purpose of being here, but along the way we get little glimpses. A set of beings with no ego, no purpose other than to serve God volunteered to help us remember why we are here. They stepped forward to be our closest guides and guardians in this universe of physical beings. Our Guardian Angels are there to guide us, to help us remember that connection to the Angelic Realms, to God, and to our life purpose contract that we signed before we came here.

As beautiful sparks of divine light we energetically move around this world and every so often those of us who have chosen to bump into our Guardian Angels form a collision so beautiful that it creates a beautiful energetic Aura of colours so perfect that they reflect throughout our lives, so that we are never the same again. When we invite Angels into our lives we can never close the door on ignorance ever again. We embark upon a karma contract that allows us to manifest wonderful opportunities and people into our lives. If we stop, breathe, and allow ourselves to feel the wonders that surround us we start to realise that as we work with Angels that there is no such word as "coincidence" in our lives. There is only karmic attraction, sometimes known as the law of attraction – that which we give out, we receive back.

My Angels show me the answer to questions through varied means known as the four Clairs (which I will explain later) and it is by tuning into these feelings, emotions, intuitions, or vibes that I see the life I signed up for, that my Angels want me to live. Through this the true joy of being starts to manifest into my life and work. They send inspiration to us through thoughts and feelings. In the hundreds of classes that I have taken many people tell me that the Angels do not want to work with them, because they cannot see the Angels. The ability to see them is a very small part of working with Angels, it is when we use all of their gifts that we truly start to see the power and love of the Angelic realms.

As a child I used to see colours around people and as an inquisitive person I was fascinated to find these colours corresponded to their emotions. I used to see beautiful sparkling lights with certain people, and as I accepted these lights I started to see beautiful pillars of light behind people, and eventually these started to become Angels. I think that the Angels are cautious so that they do not scare people, and so they give us the gifts and visions we can cope with at the point we are at in our lives.

Please believe me when I tell you that your Angels are there waiting for you to get in touch and to communicate with you. There was a person in my class who told the Angels that she was willing to work with them, but they needed to send her a sign. Every morning there was a pink feather on the pillow beside her. She threw it out, after all she wanted a white feather, as that was what the books she had read told her to watch out for. The next morning, another pink feather, again it was thrown out. This continued for several days until our next class and she told us that her Angels were ignoring her – I asked if there was anything strange that had happened and so she shared about the feathers. It turns out that she had been asking the Angels about love – and after all pink is the colour of love. Angels give us signs to light the way; we just need to be able to see them in the darkness of life.

I have always felt truly blessed in life that my mother loved and supported me when I talked about Angels, Faeries, and Spirits. She actively encouraged me to use the gifts given to me by God and the Angels to help myself and the people I came into contact with. For example, I remember once when I was asked to do a radio interview. The person who was interviewing me kept trying to make little of my beliefs and the fact that Angels exist. He asked some callers to ring in and give their opinions, and I was to comment on them. I prayed and asked Archangel Michael for courage, Archangel Uriel to give me wisdom, Archangel Raphael to guide my words to be healing to everyone who heard me, and Archangel Gabriel to make what I said clear, concise, and easy to understand. To the surprise of the interviewer everyone who phoned in wanted to share a beautiful story about Angelic intervention. Although they didn't know it they were my Angelic intervention and they gave me the faith to continue and finish the interview. Normally the interviewer would thank me at the end. He just walked away as his co-workers congratulated me. Now that is what I call divine intervention.

The Archangels

These strong, beautiful energies belong to the first choir of Angels and they care for created beings, especially for mankind and their gift of freewill. I find working with the Archangels protective yet healing, comforting yet powerful, and intense yet light-hearted. Whenever my prayer needs extra energy or I have a specific project or purpose that I am working on I call upon the Archangels to help me.

The major four Archangels are associated with the major points of a compass (compass of life illustrated later). This is important to know as when we are working with the Archangels we can invoke them in the correct orientation. Likewise, when I get in my car to set out for the day I always consider north to be the front of the car and invoke the Archangels around my vehicle, keeping my Guardian Angels inside with me. In the Angel Energist programme we use twenty major Archangels, but I use many more than this as I always like to call upon the correct Archangel for whatever I am working on.

I find to start with that the major four Archangels are enough to learn to work with at the beginning of our spiritual journey. We will discuss these Archangels, what their area of expertise is, and how to call on them in our work. However, sometimes the simplest approach is the best – my Mum has a chart of the Archangels in the kitchen to aid her if she needs to call upon them. Nevertheless she always calls upon Archangel Michael for everything. Her explanation – "He always sends the right person for the job". Enough said.

Archangel Uriel is the Guardian of the North and his name means "God is light" or "fire of God". He is the Archangel that I associate with great wisdom and is the first Archangel I call upon when I am studying or learning something new. I often see Archangel Uriel clairvoyantly holding a lamp as he illuminates the truth of situations. He holds the key to the library of the Acheshic Records and therefore the complete knowledge of the human race from the dawn of time. His Aura colour is sunshine yellow, and you can colour breathe his yellow energy to communicate with Archangel Uriel and gain insight from him. I remember I was studying for an exam for a nine week course I had to complete for work. I sat in the room I was staying in the morning of the exam and called upon Archangel Uriel and asked for his help with my knowledge for the course as I had done no studying and the exam was an hour away. Every page I "randomly" opened of my folder was in the exam and I passed with 98%. It's wonderful to know that there is a universal knowledge there to tap into in time of need. You just need to remember that when you take yourself into that energy space of the Angel within and work alongside the Archangels that the miraculous is a constant companion in your life.

Archangel Raphael is the Guardian of the East and his name means "God heals". He is the Archangel most strongly associated with physical and emotional healing. I would never presume to think that any of the healing that I do comes from myself; after all I am merely a conduit that links heaven to earth. An accurate way to view yourself in sessions where you are conducting a healing is to see Archangel Raphael standing flowing energy from heaven's choirs into your Angel within and then the energy flowing through your Angelic self and into the person's inner Angel that you are healing. From Angel – through Angel – to Angel. I use Archangel Raphael every day to ensure that the words that I speak are healing to myself and to others, and also so that I can send healing to every situation that I find myself in. Archangel Raphael is also great as a travel buddy as he is known as the patron of travellers. As I pack my bags for wherever I am going I always ensure that I pack Archangel Raphael to ensure that my bags get to my destination with me. His Aura colour is a beautiful emerald green, and you can breathe this Aura colour or surround a person, place, or situation with it to bring healing to it.

Archangel Michael is the best known of all the Archangels and if you ask a person to name an Archangel I would waiver a crystal the person would name him. Archangel Michael's name means "He who looks like God" and he works on many different levels and on many different energy levels. He is the leader of the middle choir of Angels known as the Virtues and also leads a group of Angels that is called his Band of Mercy. His Aura colour is a deep vibrant purple and he is associated with releasing negativity and fear from your life and the planet. I use Archangel Michael for protection, life purpose issues, and psychic development. He is the fix-it Angel and I have used him on many occasions to fix my computer and in particular my printer. My printer had decided not to work since a power cut when it had been on and my brother Simon who is very technically minded had looked at it and declared it to be energetically dead. Not to be discouraged I put two black tourmaline crystals on the printer and laid my hands on it, surrounding it with Archangel Michael's vibrant purple energy. I asked Archangel Michael to help heal it's components and allow them to make connections again. The next morning when I went to where my computer is the printer was working and continued to do so for some time after that. When we ask Archangel Michael to fix electrical goods remember that they are component based and that generally when they stop working that the electrical pathways are confused and no longer make connections – ask Archangel Michael to mend these pathways. Heal the cause of the problem, not the problems that it has manifested.

I would like to share a story with you about Archangel Michael. I was working with a friend of mine to help a person who had energy problems with his home. I had called upon Archangel Michael to keep me protected, as I always do when I am involved in spirit retrieval work. At the end of our work he offered to take us to a local forest where there were megalithic structures. While my friend was examining one of these my attention was captured by something moving in the forest. I walked in a little and saw a magnificent stag. I had my camera in my hand and took several pictures of the beautiful animal. When I returned to the group I told them about seeing this stag and the gentleman who had taken us there told me there were no deer in the forest and asked me where I saw it. I pointed to where it had been and he again said that there was no deer in the forest, but I was pointing to the south. Thinking nothing more if it, we left. When I was reviewing the pictures that I had taken, there in the picture was an Angel mist. When I told my brother this story he pointed out to me that the stag was the shamanic symbol of the south. As I have previously mentioned, so is Archangel Michael and when you look at the picture I'm sure you'll agree he was definitely with me that day!

Archangel Gabriel is a wonderful energy to work with and her name means "God is my strength". She is the Guardian of the west and completes the four major

Archangels. She has an energetically dual function. Her first function is related to female issues and pregnancy. Archangel Gabriel should be called upon to heal female complaints, to help people with conception issues, and the pregnancy that follows. If you are pregnant or know someone who is pregnant surround that person with Archangel Gabriel's beautiful copper gold energy. You will find that the pregnancy and childbirth will go a lot more smoothly and she also aids with morning sickness. Her other function is with communication and artistic projects. I never give a workshop without asking that Archangel Gabriel help me communicate clearly with the Angelic realms, bringing forward clear, concise, and healing information. I feel that this is why I never give the same workshop twice —as the people are different and therefore what they need to hear is different.

The Archangels are the most wonderful energies to work with and bring into our lives. I would visualise their colour around myself or the people I wish to help and see the person, place, or situation healed or helped. Whereas our Guardian Angels only work with individual charges, the Archangels can work with thousands of different charges at once, or work towards helping thousands of people with the one agenda or purpose. For example Archangel Ariel is wonderful for environmental work, while Archangel Raguel is a constant companion to groups of friends and also the work environment where his energy helps calm and regulate emotions and allows all viewpoints to be heard. These beings of light are not just there to help us, but also to be included among our most loyal and trusted friends who we can let in to every area of our lives.

There are Angels for every area of our lives, but to amplify this energy there is also the Archangels who add focus and intent to this energy, and as I always tell my practitioners – why only use your own personal Angels to complete every task when you have a Heavenly host at your wingtips?

The following five exercises will help you to connect to your Angelic guides in your everyday life.

Exercise One: The power of breath

A common trait in all living organisms is the need to breathe. Plants and animals alike need to breathe to live, yet as life has become more stressful humans have forgotten how to. If you watch a baby sleeping their tummy moves when they breathe; or a person receiving a spiritual healing, again you can start to see their stomach moving up and down. When I am conducting a healing I find myself doing pranic breathing – this is when you find yourself sighing to move energy. People always feel so relaxed after a treatment, as I find that I remove so much negative energy and replace it with positive that it is almost like an energy transfusion. You can physically see them starting to breathe properly as the negative energy is removed.

This exercise is simple. Take in a deep breath and watch as you abdomen expands, and then let the breath out slowly through your teeth, so you make an "sssssss" sound. Do this 5 times and notice how you feel more relaxed after each breath.

This technique helps to remove toxic carbon dioxide from your body and gets more oxygen in. Also it makes you breathe through your diaphragm. Most of us only use the top of our lungs, which is the smallest area. We therefore have less oxygen in our blood, and then add carbonated soft drinks and we start to feel very tired and less likely to want to do meditation. By using more of our lungs, we get more oxygen in and start to feel more awake and encouraged to fit more into the day.

As we breathe we start to manifest people, places, and situations in our lives. Angels can only enter, intervene, and assist in changing our lives if we ask them – this is the law of free will that Angels work by. We must ask to receive. We contact and communicate with all Angelic beings, including the one inside us when we breathe and listen.

Breathe is a divine gift given to us by the Goddess Mother Earth when we are born and returned as a sacred part of our soul to God or Father Sky when we cross back into the world of spirit.

Exercise Two: The four Clairs

I used to dislike my name when I was little and wished I had a more exotic name. When I had first heard that we chose our names and whisper them to our mothers before we are born, I fully disagreed. That was until I started my Angelic journey and was introduced to the concept of the four Clairs. I found that I had indeed chosen my name, and found myself falling in love with it when at a training event someone came up to me, and told me that they thought my name was beautiful and suited my work.

Here are the definitions of the four Clairs:

Clairvoyance: "Clear seeing" through your minds eye, physical eyes or dreams.

Clairsentience: "Clear feeling" through physical and emotional feelings; also a sense of smell.

Clairaudience: "Clear hearing" through words in your head, outside your head, songs you hear.

Claircognizance: "Clear thinking" – through a knowingness without knowing how you know; ideas and revelations that come through inspiration.

This exercise can take five minutes or as much time as you want to put into it. Close your eyes and allow yourself to breathe. As you do so, spend a minute thinking about all the things you know for sure about your life and yourself. For example: My name is Rebecca. My hair colour is dark. Introduce your everyday self to your higher self. Listing all the things you know about yourself uses Claircognizance.

Next using Clairaudience, spend a minute hearing all that is going on around you. Whether you are sitting listening to the ocean, or birds singing, or in the silence of your own home – spend time listening, truly listening.

What do you hear??

We now move onto the gift of Clairsentience. Spend the next minute feeling what is going on around you. Feel what it is to be you. Feel what is going on around you. Feel the temperature around you, and the air around you.

The fourth Clair is Clairvoyance. At this time I ask that you look at yourself using your third eye. Scan yourself and see yourself through your Angels eyes. See your true spiritual self. What do you look like? What is different between the "real" you and that what you see in the mirror?

Finally, I ask that you spend the last minute sitting quietly in your "own skin", sitting with yourself and being at peace. After all, how do we think that we can sense that we are in the presence of Angels when we do not know what it is to sense ourselves first.

Write the results of this exercise in your Angel diary that you will take with you every step along this stage of life's pathway. As you continue to use this exercise you will find that your "psychic" ability will expand and you will be more aware of synchronised events around you. You will be able to start to hear the sounds of mother earth that were not speaking to you before, start to see Angel lights sparkling from the corners of your eyes and colours around yourself and others, and be able to distinguish different energies around you as you go through daily life. All of these will reconnect you to your Guardian Angels and also to the Angel within that is connected to God.

Exercise Three: The Angel Diary

When I was younger every January 1st I started a new diary, and typically this diary lasted about two weeks. After this I became bored, found I had nothing exciting enough to write in it, and generally left it beside my bed.

I want to tell you now an Angel Diary is not like this. It does not have to be filled with pages of exciting Angel encounters, although with Angels one never knows..... This is a book for you and your Guardian Angels only to read. It is a book filled with Angel dreams, encounters, aspirations, manifestation lists, feathers that you find, articles that you read that speak to you, and a host of other experiences that you will discover when connected to the Angelic realms. The most important point is that it is a means of communication between you, your Angels, and your inner Angel.

It is a book that can be filled in once a day, once a month, or once a year. Whenever it feels right to you. My diary tends to have a string of experiences, lie dormant for a while, and then another flurry of activity. It depends what is going on in my life, and how much time I have to nourish my Angel within.

The first step is to buy a book that feels right to you. It can be any shape or size. Then, I always like to decorate mine as I go. I stick Angel pictures, articles, white feathers that my Angels leave me etc into it as I go. It is unique to the user. I suggest that everyone starts one and writes any dreams they have when they wake up, anything you wish to manifest into your life, any co-incidences, synchronicities, or events that you attribute to Angelic intervention in it. As you read back over what you have written in it, you will start to see patterns and Angelic hints emerging as you do. When we are in the middle of a storm or crisis in our lives, we cannot always see the advice that is being offered. By looking at this advice emerging through our diaries we can start to appreciate what is being gently whispered to us by our Angels.

This is why when I was choosing a name for my Angel business I chose Angelic Whispers – this is what my Angels do to me on a daily basis, whisper in my thoughts, feelings, and ear. This is also the way they share their advice, so all that they whisper to you should go into the diary, for you to reflect on and ultimately bring into your life.

Exercise Four: Affirmations

If you have never used them before the next step along your Angel pathway and learning to communicate and work with the Angel within is the use of Affirmations. These statements can be as simple or as complex as you wish to make them. I personally prefer my affirmations to be simple and that I am able to connect with them at a spiritual level. If you wish to make your own affirmation, here are a few guidelines on how to create them:

*An affirmation should always be **positive**, focusing only on the positive within ourselves and situations we are in.*

*It should be in the **present tense** – after all we are living, breathing souls. We live for today alone – the future is built on our today's.*

*An affirmation is a personal contract that we are embarking on with our souls – so be honest and keep it **personal**. Don't forget our Angels want us to take care of ourselves first and then start to work for other people.*

*Think about the **language** of you affirmation – it should be simple, clear, and you should be able to connect with it. Don't try to manifest situations into your life that you do not want because you feel it's what you should be asking for – ask for situations that are real and important to you.*

Now that you have an affirmation you should connect with it – feel or visualise the affirmation being brought into your life. Read it out loud to your Guardian Angels and allow it to surround and permeate your Angel. Write it out and leave it around the house in places that you will see often. Use this affirmation for 21 days and write in your Angel diary all the events that have come into your life that you feel are related to this affirmation.

If you could not decide an affirmation to use, here are some of my favourites that I always feel have a special resonance with Incarnated Angels:

I allow myself to attract joy, peace, and happiness into my life daily

I am only responsible for myself at this time in my life

I have the power within to live
my dreams daily

I attract only friends who are
spiritually minded like myself

I am worthy to give and receive love

I'm sure as you read those affirmations that at least one if not all of them pulled at your Angel within, and that she was saying "That's the one" or "That is so true". Only use one affirmation at a time until you have added it's true meaning to your spiritual tool belt. For all lightworkers out there the affirmations that I have included above are some of the hardest you will ever work with, but they are the most rewarding – after all if you achieve attracting joy, peace, love, and worthy friends into your life imagine what your life would be like................

Another interesting way to find the affirmation you wish to work with is to make them into your own deck of Angel cards. As I encounter wonderful phrases and affirmations through my life I write them in my Angel diary, but also write them on a piece of card. All these pieces of card are popped into a velvet bag, and I use them as my own personal Angel oracle – after all these words spoke to me for a reason, therefore they are special to me and my life. This is a cheap and wonderful communication method for working with the Angelic realms.

I would advise everyone to start this today and in no time at all you will have a faithful and accurate guidance tool. I sometimes use these cards in my workshops instead of the bought variety – and I have found that people are more responsive to them, as they start to share what they feel they mean with others. Without knowing it people are starting to give Angel readings without the fear factor coming into play. Giving and receiving Angel readings is a beautiful and divine gift from the Angels, and they want more spiritually motivated lightworkers guiding others. Therefore now is the perfect time to start to polish these gifts from the Angels.

When I started professional readings I was always terrified and tried to soften sometimes blunt messages from the Angels. Over time I have learnt to give the information as it comes to me, without the rough edges taken off. We are all merely a willing pair of hands here to help in God's plan.

Exercise Five: Noticing the signs!

Throughout my career working with and teaching about Angels, the biggest complaint I have encountered from the human race about their Angelic counterparts is that they do not receive signs from their Angels. I have to put this myth right once and for all – they DO send us signs – we just don't SEE them. Most of us walk through life and don't see what is right under our noses. We see everything clearly for our friends, but not for ourselves. I want to outline some of the most common ways our feathered friends try to get our attention:

1. **White feathers** in unusual places. These feathers do

not have to be white, they can be any colour or any size, but they normally appear when we need them and in a place where you would not expect to find a feather. I mostly get them blowing into my face as my Angels know that I normally walk around with my head in the clouds.

2. **Hearing your name being called** in the distance, but there is no-one there. This normally happens on the edge of sleep, as we have given our rational brain some time off. You normally wake up wanted to speak to them, but when you can't see them go back to sleep. In future have a chat with your Angels; it's a wonderful time to ask them for answers you are seeking.

3. Our Angels also visit us in **dreams**. That is why it is so valuable to write down our dreams when we wake up. Do not let these precious insights and messages fall away into the grey area between sleep and wake.

4. **Nephomancy** is divination through studying clouds. Angels send us messages when we take the time to look up at the skies. I love to photograph clouds, and frequently see Angelic shapes and animals in clouds.

5. **Music**. This is a wonderful mode of communication from the Angels. Whether you hear a song with the word Angel throughout it, or there is that one line of a song that plays in you head all day – listen up because you have received a sign through Angel FM. Also people report hearing beautiful music when there is no radio or TV on.

6. **Pennies from heaven**. We are all unique and receive

different signs, but I always receive 5 pence coins from my Angels. I now know to look if it is a heads or tails when I pick them up – I like to think heads for yes and tails for no to whatever question is on my mind that day. I have a jar I put them all into and give them to charity.

7. **Angel lights and colours**. Angels show themselves to us as flashes of light that we see (normally out of the corner of your eye) and colours that surround people or pets. We call these Angel lights and these are frequently caught on cameras at special events – most people now call them orbs.

Many of the physical signs that we receive, such as feathers or coins, you can put on your Angel Altar as a symbol that you have heard your Angels and know that they are with you.

An **Angel Altar** is easy to set up in your home, I know that mine is a central part of the home and changes regularly depending on my mood or what is going on in my life, or what I want to attract into my life. Making your Altar is like making your Angel Diary – it is a connection between the physical you and the divine you. Here are a few suggestions that you can put on your altar:

Start with a cloth. Pick a colour
corresponding to an Archangel you feel an affinity to,
or a simple white cloth is
representative of Guardian Angels.
Place a candle on it to represent
that you work in the light of creation.
An Angel on the altar shows the energies
that you are aligned to.
Crystals or shells bring in the
elemental kingdom of the Faeries.
Wood or natural seeds such as pine cones or chestnuts bring
in the energy of Mother Earth.
Anything else you wish to bring to your Angels attention.
You can place a photograph of someone who needs healing,
or a map of a country that needs healing. It's your space
and your choice.

This area gives you a focal point to use to work with the Angels. Keep the energy clear and don't allow it to get cluttered with things that you do not wish to manifest into your life. For example if you leave a bill on the altar and do not ask for your financial situation to be healed, then you will probably find more bills coming your way!

I found as I started to bring these first steps into my life that I started to allow my Angels to offer guidance in all areas of my life at all times. Also I found that if I told my Angels what the end result was that I wanted in my life, then I would step aside and let them do what they knew was best for me. Following the first few encounters I have never questioned my Angels and I now know the blessing behind unanswered prayers.

Allow yourself to revel in these first techniques before you move on, knowing that your Angels are guiding your way like beacons in the dark drawing you into the safe harbour of their love and protection. It is always a comfort to me knowing that I am safely held in the palm of God's hand through the loving ministries of his Angels.

The following part of this section of the book introduces you to the concept of your auric field, how it interacts with your physical body, the influence of crystals, and nature elementals we interact with daily and seasonally.

The Aura

The human Aura is a constantly changing energy field that surrounds our bodies from the moment we are conceived to the moment we return to the world of spirit. In truth I have seen the remains of an Aura around those whose souls have left their body, as their Aura had been so strong in life. When I first started to "see" Auras around people I would see a faint white outline around them that moved with them. As my spiritual sight progressed I started to see colours, and eventually I could see Angels and guides in the energy field surrounding people's Auras. I personally feel that one way in which to communicate with our own Guardian Angels, the Angel within, and other people's Angels is to learn to see, feel, and communicate with our own and other beings Auras. I specifically say the word "beings" as all living things have Auras – from the flowers and trees in the ground, to our beloved pets, to the birds of the air. They all have their own unique energy pattern, and it is this pattern that we begin to see, feel, and communicate with as we start to open ourselves to the world outside our five senses. I will not call it our sixth sense, as we have so many more that six, and as we progress along our life's journey we start to encounter each one magically hidden by our Angels for us to discover and start to use when we are ready.

When I see a human Aura it usually stretches about an arms length from the body and the same above and below it. It moves with the person and is made up of mostly white energy with colours through it. These colours change as our mood changes, and also change when we meet different people who we have an affinity with or dislike. When we meet other like-minded people our Auras stretch out to embrace them in a spiritual hug, and we instinctively know things about this person as we exchange information in this fashion. On the other hand we may meet people that we do not resonate with and our Aura pulls in tightly around us and does not exchange energy with the person and so conversation is stilted and reserved.

Our Aura is a moving extension of us, and even if we are not in touch with our spiritual self we can still determine whether a person is in integrity through Aura communication. How many times in the past did we instinctively feel that we instantly liked / disliked someone and no matter what was said afterwards we could not bring ourselves to change our first impression of them. This is why we always feel that first impressions are the most important. Now, as I go into the world I can appreciate that all people are made differently and everyone is at a different point on the spiritual evolutionary ladder. As I leave the comforting security of home I constantly ask my Guardian Angels to be with me and allow me only to meet and interact with people who are spiritually minded like myself and resonate only with the highest energies. I have found that since I have started my journeys with this Angelic protection that life's highway has become more smooth and easy to transverse.

I also find that asking my Guardian Angels to surround me with white light every morning and evening that any energy that my Aura may lose from bumping off other energy sources is replenished and my Aura restored. You do not have to find powerful words to invoke this level of protection. I find that keeping it short and simple is the best. I would normally say:

"Angels, I ask that you surround me with white light protection throughout the day".

An alternative phrase to call your Angels by your side is:

"Angels, I ask you to go before my every step this day and prepare my way with Angelic love".

As Angels are agents of freewill, as soon as you petition them for help they are only too eager and willing to provide and offer this help, and more. This protection can also be invoked for family, friends, loved ones, pets and your home. So always remember to share your Angelic love around as many beautiful beings as possible in the world.

For example, I have three dogs – two Shih Tzus (Jupiter and Oberon) and a Pekingese (Perseus). Jupiter and Oberon are the type of dogs that never leave home. They like the security of being close and knowing that you are with them. Our Perseus is somewhat of a free spirit and tends to escape when no-one is looking and runs for miles. In these situations I always ask that the Angelic foot soldiers of light walk with him and keep him safe. On one such occasion we had had junk mail delivered and Perseus was outside in the sun. The person delivering it did not close the gate properly and so he once again made his escape. When we discovered that he was gone we didn't know how long he had been out or which direction he had taken. I automatically sent a prayer up to Archangel Ariel (who works with and protects animals) and the Angelic foot soldiers of lights to keep him safe until we found him. We eventually found him – after he had crossed several major roads. Thank goodness that when he decides to wander off on his adventures he always has an Angel by his side!

I also find that white light is a very important tool in you spiritual tool belt. As I surround myself in white light, so I cleanse my Angel within with the same beautiful light and protection. It feeds the soul and purifies you from the inside out. White light incorporates all the colours of the visible spectrum, and so when we use white light we are also using the different rays of light and the Archangels that are associated with the different colours in the spectrum. This allows us to start to bring in the higher energies that are accessible to us in our every day lives.

Your Angel within and the physical body

We must remember that our body is an outward representation of our spiritual thoughts and manifestations. We are all born as beautiful children of God and as we start to grow up we still have a divine connection with God and the Angels. This starts to change as our ego finds its voice. Children between the ages of 0-9 have a tendency to tell the truth and have beautiful spiritual experiences. After this age they tend to not have as many of these experiences and they start to exhibit signs of the ego. My nephew, Kristian, was looked after by my Mum when my brother and his wife were at work and he was brought up with the knowledge and love of Angels and Faeries everywhere in his life. My Mum had a large Faerie ornament in the centre of the room. When I asked him if he had done something wrong he would go and stand beside the ornament and tell the Faeries that he was telling the truth. He instinctively knew, even at his young age, about different energies that surround and work with us; and that representations of them in the home are a potent reminder of the need to always remember to act as if we are in their presence.

Ego is not a vain and beautiful creature, instead it is there to try and make us forget our true spiritual mission and trick us into seeing ourselves as merely human beings and not spiritual beings. Through learning about the connections between our physical and spiritual bodies we are able to start to discern through clairsentience how our thoughts and experiences are affecting our bodies. Also if there is a situation in your life that you wish to release, knowing how to tap into your spiritual body can be a very important lesson. This information falls under the category of "the aura" as the aura is an extension of your spiritual body and the part that most people are familiar with.

Within the aura are areas which in my experience tend to hold issues and cellular memories from our experiences as we travel along life's pathway (Cellular memories are memories and habits that are stored in the cells of our body). Below I have included a table of these aura areas and the issues associated with them. We can release these issues to lighten our spiritual bodies and allow ourselves to move forward in our lives. When working with each area, visualise the person, place, or situation associated with what you wish to heal or release and then surround it with the healing white light of the Angels. I find that it is beneficial that as you do this to hold your forehead, in particular the area above your eyes. As this aura area is cleansed it will become harder to visualise the person, place, or situation.

Aura Areas of the body.

Also within the Aura we have **etheric cords** which are energy connections that form between people, places, and situations. We can never break cords of love which nourish us spiritually and help us in our daily life. There are, however, etheric cords which affect our lives negatively and drain us of our precious energy. I carry out energy treatments, as I can see that many physical problems are caused from the emotional over a long period of time, and so by keeping ourselves emotionally strong we are giving our bodies a better chance of staying whole and healthy. Negative etheric cords form between people through fear-based emotions such as anger, depression, loneliness, co-dependency, unforgiveness, and other negative emotions. These can form in normal relationships at any time, even alongside cords of love and devotion. They are nothing to be worried or ashamed of. They are a normal and natural part of life. By being aware of them we can remove those which do not serve or highest good, while keeping those that do. Energy runs back and forth through these tubes and can cause chronic fatigue syndrome and burn out in healers, which is why when I teach energy healing to my practitioners I always teach them to cut etheric cords to their clients following the treatment. Cords around the feet region connect a person to a physical object that they cannot part with.

Like cellular memory areas of our body, etheric cords also have certain areas associated with them.

Area of the body	Representation
Third eye chakra	Seeing the whole picture and the truth in a situation
Ear chakras	Hearing the spoken and unspoken truth in a situation
Throat chakra	Speaking your spiritual truth
Shoulders	Release burdens you carry and expectations of how you are to behave.
Heart chakra	Release your fear, negativity, and old behaviours
Spine	Helps to strengthen resolve, and heals support issues
Stomach	Helps to digest life with ease
Elimination organs	Release toxic situations from your life and soul
Hands	Allowing you to give and receive equally and in balance
Legs	Allows you to move forward and stand up for yourself

Etheric Cord Areas of the Body:

Body Area	Underlying Cause
Shoulders	Siblings
Shoulder Blades	Children
Heart Chakra	Mum / Dad
Solar Plexus	Lovers
Sides	Friendships
Lower Back	Spouse / Ex-spouse
Legs	Clients
Feet	Property / Possessions

Etheric cords clairvoyantly look an opaque, milky white colour. New relationships have a fine cord like a hair and older relationships have larger cords which are think and deep rooted like an oak tree. Etheric cords can even be connected when the other person is in the spirit world. I have been called to many clients who could not move on with their lives following a bereavement only to find that they were holding the person from moving on spiritually through the depth of their grief. Having severed the cord of dependency the clients have started to move forward with their lives. The cords of love they had to the person are unbroken and their connection to them is still strong in a healthy way.

One client had been with their terminally ill mother at the time of her passing. When her mother was near her last breath she had gotten on the bed and held her and begged her mother not to leave her. From the moment her mother had died she had had a bitter taste physically in her mouth which had left her unable to eat. Her health had declined, she lost weight, and became a prisoner in her own home when her daughter (the deceased woman's grand-daughter) called me. The woman was terrified as she had heard her deceased father calling her name and telling her to come with him every night when she went to bed. She believed that she was dying. When I went to her home I noticed her mother standing behind her. As she was telling me the story of what was happening to her I was watching the reactions of the mother in the spirit world and the daughter in the physical world. When she was telling me about her father calling her at night – the mother was pointing to herself. I asked her if she was called after her mother. It turns out that she was the fourth daughter born and was indeed named after her mother. The deceased mother had stayed with her daughter as she had begged her to, but to do this she had corded to her and formed what I call a piggy-back effect. In essence she was living off her daughter's energy. The taste was what the mother had been experiencing leading up to her passing, and as their energies were combined she was now experiencing this also. Her father was calling his wife to come to the light every night, but a promise had been made and the mother stayed with her child. I broke the cords of dependency and the taste immediately disappeared and the woman was able to eat and gradually started to live a normal and healthy life.

Angels and their Crystal Friends

Crystals, like Angels, are a thread that unites all cultures across the planet throughout time. If Angels are the golden thread that pulls all religions together, then Crystals are the silver one that if we hold onto it tightly will pull ever person and culture on mother earth together as God intended us to be. If we look at crystals and organic matter from which life derives on the earth, you will find that it is crystalline in structure. The beautiful quartz crystal is made from silica, and this is one of the most common compounds found on earth.

I work with many different and diverse energies that enable me to work as a complete spiritual being and allow me to connect to my Angel within. I work with Angelic and Faerie energies which elevate my own personal attunements so that I can communicate freely with these beings of light and love. I also work with earth energies which ground me in this time and space, so that I do not become too dreamy and float away with the Angels. We call the successful melding of this energy work the rainbow bridge. We connect heaven and earth and walk this bridge with compassion, truth, honour, and joy.

As a spiritual being I need my head to be elevated above events which do not serve my highest good and stay in communication with my Angels and my feet to be firmly embedded in Mother Nature or Gaia. A rainbow has seven colours, which when we contemplate it corresponds to our seven major chakras. It is no co-incidence or surprise that nature and the human body correspond in divine perfection. Everything in the universe is in divine alignment from the heavens above to the earth and the life on it, to the oceans and the life within. When we start to realise and appreciate this, we then start to let the rainbow bridge flow from us in all directions of time and from there we start to walk it on a daily basis to increase our spiritual evolution process.

Each soul on this earth has an ancient crystal knowledge buried within them that enables them to communicate with the elemental kingdom and re-connect themselves with the powerful rhythm of life that pulses around us in cosmic and divine alignment. Each of the Archangels has specific crystals associated with them, as do our chakras; and it is no mistake that these overlap – once again in divine order. Whether we wear crystal jewellery, carry a touch stone, or use the crystal for healing purposes the most important aspect of using crystals in your everyday life is to use breath and intention. As long as you create the energy with breath and set your intention for the highest good then the crystal energy will amplify your intention and add its own unique energy to the cause.

I always smile when I hear the statement "As above, so below". To me it means "As in heaven so also on earth" and when I start to mediate further on it I always feel that Angelic characteristics are reflected on the earth in crystal form. An Angel always offers you honest, trustworthy advice that is for your highest good – as a crystal does when you sit down and channel a message from it. Therefore we do not have far to look for an earthly manifestation of heaven when we start to bring crystals into our lives and homes. Therefore a beautiful clear quartz crystal is a wonderful aid to help you contact the Angel within your spiritual body. A rainbow is often seen inside the clear quartz when held to the light, and once again brings in the power and significance of the rainbow in our lives.

I channelled this beautiful message from a clear quartz crystal point, and it is a message I would like to share with all Earth Angels out there:

"From the heavens above to the oceans beneath are the realms of love, creation, and imagination. What you believe you shall receive. What you know will be your pathway. What you learn will be your future. The power of thought, word, and deed is the all encompassing world of reality. Be pure in all these aspects and remember always to look within your heart where your real inspiration lives".

This shows me that when we tap into the elemental energies of nature we start to appreciate that we are in perfect alignment with nature. We create our own lives through our thought, word, and action. How often have we spoken something in jest to discover that it manifests? The clear quartz crystal also shared with me that if we align ourselves with the energy of crystals that we allow crystal light to shine out as a beacon to others and to other parts of your soul allowing you to start a new alignment through celestial guides.

As you work with these crystal guides you will find your psychic ability increasing dramatically. It is impossible to work with such high vibrational energies and not become increasingly aware of energies around you.

Crystal Layouts

I use crystal layouts on myself and others to align to the energy of my Guardian Angels and also the Archangels. A crystal layout is a particular pattern or layout of crystal on or around the body to rebalance our body or Auras energy or to connect to the energy of Angels. It does not require you to stay long in the crystal layouts to feel the benefits. Five to ten minutes is ample time to connect to the Angels and / or yourself.

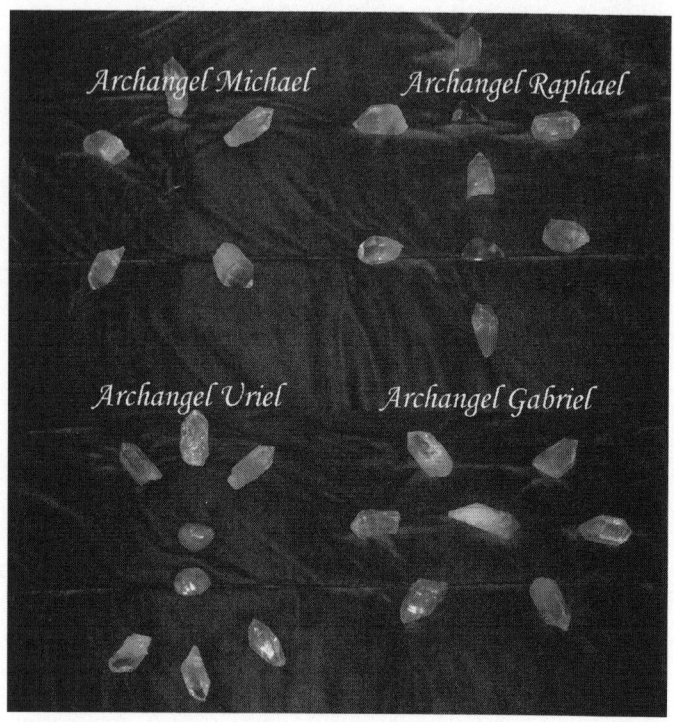

Archangel Michael   Archangel Raphael

Archangel Uriel   Archangel Gabriel

The first layout that I wish to share with you is the **Guardian Angel layout.** Lie down and place seven rose quartz crystals on you, one on each Chakra position. Then take seven quartz crystal points and place three on each side of the head on the floor, pointing outwards. The last crystal point is placed at the top of your head pointing up. A black obsidian is placed in between your feet to ground you. The rose quartz is a crystal of universal and unconditional love that brings compassion into all aspects of our lives.

The **Archangel Michael layout** uses a sugilite crystal and five quartz crystal points. Put on some calming music and lie down. The sugilite is placed on the heart Chakra and the five quartz crystal points placed in the shape of a five pointed star around it. Sugilite is a crystal that opens the gates to channelling divine information. This crystal layout can also be used for courage, life purpose, and protection as Archangel Michael is associated with all these areas.

The **Archangel Raphael layout** uses two malachite crystals and seven quartz crystal points. Find a calming energy space and put on some crystal or chanting music in the background and lie down. The malachite crystals are placed on your heart Chakra and solar plexus Chakra. The quartz points are placed one on either side of the malachite pointing out, one above the heart Chakra malachite pointing up, one below the solar plexus malachite pointing down, and the last point is between the two malachite pointing up. Malachite is a crystal associated with healing and pain relief. This crystal layout can also be used for healing emotions and situations we find ourselves in.

The **Archangel Gabriel layout** uses a citrine crystal and six quartz crystal points. Put on some pan pipe music and lie down in this relaxing energy. The citrine is placed on your heart Chakra. The quartz points are placed in a figure of eight around it – three on each side of your body. Citrine is the crystal of abundance and the figure of eight represents the infinity symbol, linking you to infinite new possibilities and abundance in all areas of your life.

The **Archangel Uriel layout** requires two sunstones and six quartz crystal points. A sunstone is placed on the third eye Chakra and the other is placed on the heart Chakra, linking your head and heart together. Three quartz points are placed in a fan above the head, and the other three quartz points are placed in a fan below the feet; like the suns rays projection out from your body. Sunstone is a crystal associated with happiness, and self-worth. When linked to the energy of Archangel Uriel it allows us to tap into inner knowledge and our Akashic records.

Below is a crystal Chakra guide to use when balancing your Chakras. This can be done using a crystal layout on the body. You can lie down and ask someone to place the crystals in the table on your Chakra point (or you can do it yourself). Lie in this **Chakra rainbow layout** for five to ten minutes or until you feel energised and you body's natural energy grid recharged.

Chakra	ChakraColour	Stone	Archangel
Crown	Violet	ClearQuartz	Raziel
ThirdEye	Indigo	Amethyst	Michael
Throat	Blue	Sodalite	Jeremiel
Heart	Green	RoseQuartz	Raphael/Jophiel
SolarPlexus	Yellow	Citrine	Uriel
Sacral	Orange	Carnelian	Gabriel
Root	Red	Hematite	Zadkiel

Crystals – a basic healing kit.

Crystals work by affecting our body on a physical and emotional level. Different people choose crystals that speak to them. Experience has taught me that crystals choose and find me, very rarely do I get a say in the matter! Some of the ways we choose crystals are:

- **Colour**. The vibrational rate of colour interacts and heals our body in both the physical and emotional layers of our Aura. It is a powerful healing tool and many people choose their crystals by colour rather than by any other means.

- **Sensation**. By holding a crystal in the palm of your hand the crystal will invoke a sensation or feeling inside you. You will either feel that this is the crystal you need to use, or you feel nothing – this will let you know that the crystal is waiting for another owner. This method is also used in vibrational crystal healing in which a healing is carried out using crystals that have all geographically came from the same country of origin IE- using only crystals from Brazil or Africa.

- **A Crystal directory**. This is a book filled with crystals, their functions, and how to use them. These are useful at the beginning of your crystalline journey, but as you progress you will find that each author has differing functions and it quickly gets confusing. That is why I truly believe that you should use your Inner Angel and intuition to work with the crystal kingdom.

The following crystals are essential to have in your crystal healing kit:

I have picked the following crystals to correspond with the Chakra crystal, to give them dual purpose for you to use in all areas of your life.

Quartz – The beautiful quartz crystal is made from silica, and this is one of the most common compounds found on earth. It is a universal communication stone and a powerful healer which aids clarity to situations, enhances meditation, and focuses your mind.

Amethyst – It is the general fix-it-all stone used in healing and spiritual development. You can use amethyst as a powerful healer, a stone of protection, or a stone to sooth and cleanse.

Sodalite – This stone is wonderful for communication. It allows you to combine and balance your natural intellect with intuition to help yourself and others through Angelic communication.

Rose Quartz – This beautiful stone is generally considered to encourage love and harmony in your personal, professional, and spiritual life.

Citrine – This is the stone of abundance – remembering that abundance affects every area of your life and is not specific to your financial situation. This is a stone of light and cheerful energy, bringing the energy of creation into your life.

Carnelian – This is a powerful stone of protection. It can be used to cleanse people's energy fields and other crystals. It can be used to aid the lifting of emotions and brings the energy of courage into your life.

Haematite – This crystal is a stone of survival. It is a wonderful calming and grounding expert and is most widely used for blood conditions and pains in the extremities.

As your crystal family extends and more come to work with you then you will find yourself gaining knowledge through working with them. For many years I have seen beautiful energy fields around crystals, and as I work with crystals for healing on people, animals, and places I can see the energy of my clients changing in response to these wonderful energies.

Crystal energies have been working with us through the major periods in history and now as we move into the new age of enlightenment more of these precious friends are coming forward to share their knowledge and peace with us. Some examples of these new age crystals are: kunzite, sugilite, serephenite, and the wonderful lemurian seed crystals.

Your Angel Within and Water

As I stand in the rain I am very aware of Archangel energies surrounding me, as they associate closely with the element of rain. I always ask that as the rain falls down on me that the Angels and the Archangels that I work with rain blessings into my life. Mother Nature or Gaia as some cultures call her reminds us with every act that we must take care what we are doing in our everyday lives. The planet is a living, breathing being – the oceans are her lungs and as we pollute them we should look to ourselves and our body to see the effects. If we did not give a plant enough water it would die, yet we rarely think about the quality or quantity of water that we put into our own bodies and the effect that it has on our body as a whole. The experiments of Dr. Masaru Emoto should give us all food for thought about the quality of the water we drink and how our own emotions influence it. Up to 60% of the human body weight is composed of water. Humans are emotional creatures and the majority of people that I have surveyed in my classes tell me that their emotions change with the changing cycles of the moon – just like the oceans, but our emotions are the oceans that flow inside of us.

Water can take on three forms: solid, liquid, and gas. It can be soaked up by different substances and interchange between its different forms through processes such as evaporation, condensation, freezing, melting etc. It is different to every other liquid and floats when it is in its frozen state – which is why we have icebergs. Water is found on Earth in all three forms. This is because Earth is a very special planet with just the right range of temperatures and air pressures. I had never really taken the time to appreciate water for all its unique traits, until I was standing in the rain, letting it run down my face, being at one with nature and contemplating why the Archangels associate so closely with the element of rain.

Then, as always, my Angels provided me with the answer. Every living being on earth needs water to survive. The same is true for our soul. Our Angels feed us with the spiritual food that we need to progress along life's pathway. The Archangels water us daily through divine guidance, divine timing, and intuition. They are our constant companions and that is why, when we may turn our back on all other guides in our life we are never able to turn away from our Angels. We may turn our back on their advice, we can pretend not to hear them as they whispers in our dreams and in our ears. However, we can never remove them or their constant guidance from our life.

Every living being on this planet has a Guardian Angel watching over it, from the Faeries watching over nature to the Angels watching over the human race, to the Principalities watching over nations throughout our world. We are all spiritual beings and no matter how hard we may try to hide from the rain, it still has a way of finding us – whether we follow our children as they splash laughingly in puddles, or find that in the darkest corner we are hiding in, that annoying drip still manages to find us. We were made waterproof for a reason – so that we could join with our heavenly allies in appreciating the wonder of Mother Nature and her power to wipe away impurities and fears.

Water cleanses, it is what is used to baptise children into belief systems, and it is what two thirds of your body is made up from. As beings of water we are governed by the tidal rhythms of the waves, and as such our life moves in rhythms – highs and lows. It is only through allowing your Angels and the Archangels to rain blessings into your life on a daily basis that we can surf along the top of life's ocean as it breathes new life into all we touch.

Therefore I ask that as you honour your Angel within that you start to contemplate what you put into it. At this stage of your journey your Angels are not asking you to make big changes in your diet that you find difficult to adjust to – they ask that you start with one of the basic requirements of life – water. They ask that you continue to replenish and cleanse your body with it, and also that you consider the quality of the water that you take into your body. At times I like to fill bottles of water from natural springs and wells, or buy a brand that I feel resonates with me (just hold the bottle to your heart chakra and sense what it tells you). Alternatively you can put a crystal friend in the water to elevate its energy, being careful to remove the crystal prior to drinking the water, or even collect rainwater (depending on where you live).

Start to consult with your Angel within and allow that inner voice to guide you.

The River of Life

While I was thinking about our relationship with water my Angels guided me to share with you the analogy that they have given me in regard to you, your Angels, and the river of life. Your Angels view our lives as a constantly moving stream that we must navigate along to bring us to our spiritual enlightenment. At the start of the river it is a small stream, easy to traverse and with no major problems or obstacles stopping us. We then join the river proper and as we start to move along this we discover obstacles and fish that make our route less smooth. As we grow we learn how to move around these obstacles, and in some cases as we grow older we learn to meet these obstacles as equals and instead of having to move around them we sidestep each other.

As the river is more mature then there are minor rivulets off it that will lead us on exciting new journeys, but ultimately we will have to listen to the advice of our Angels and come back onto our original course that we started on so many years ago. As we listen to our Angels and start to move along our original path we realise that the river is going up a hill or a mountain to the summit and our life is filled with different types of challenges, and that the material worries of our youth are replaced with issues such as life purpose and spiritual evolution where we are moving closer to the river source. Eventually when we reach the top and reach the source of all energy and power – that beautiful being that we refer to as God, then we know that we are in perfect alignment with our Angels and we will know the bliss of being with them fully.

My Angels communicate with me Clairaudiently through songs. I will start to hear music in my head, then the lyrics will start and the important lyrics that they want me to hear will play over and over again in my head. Recently when my Angels started to show me life as a river that we move along the Garth Brooks song "The River" started playing in my head and the lyrics started to flow through my head. This is one of the most natural and sensitive ways that Angels can communicate with you through the gift of Clairaudience – music has such a beautiful energy that emanates from it and therefore Angels can communicate through it and your Inner Angel can understand it perfectly.

It is so true that turbulent waters constantly throw us off course and just when we think that we can relax another wave engulfs us. The only reason for this is to test us to ensure that our hearts are pure and that when we get to the waters that we have to climb through to get to the source of life's river then we will wade through them effortlessly and step over anything that is put in our way. Our Angels are there not only to guide us but to ensure that we spiritually evolve.

Next time you are at a "crossroad" in your life, ask your Guardian Angels to show you clairvoyantly if you are in your river of life? Or trying to swim into a rivulet? Likewise when I am hit by wave upon wave in the stream I ask my Angels what the lesson is that I am missing so I can move on? We evolve as we learn and I personally would rather learn the first time rather than the third or fourth time – wouldn't you?

Working with Angels does not make your path obstacle-free, easy, and without worries. It does however allow you to see the obstacles before they materialise, it helps us to smooth our own path through our actions, and worry is nothing more than a negative prayer that does not belong in our lives. So every time worry comes along I turn it around and see the positive that my Angels want me to see, and with practice visualising your life as a river very soon you will be able to use this Angelic technique as well.

Angels and Nature

I constantly tell people to ask their Guardian Angels for help and guidance and to hand over their worries and problems to them. The same applies when we are dealing with the members of the animal kingdom. When I carry out healing on an animal I will do it with their permission first, and then working alongside their Guardian Angel – which is a Faery. As a spiritual being it is important that we work with all the energies around us. Nature surrounds us on each island of land that we live on. We are surrounded by water and the nature elements that live and work there. Our landscape is lush and green filled with airborne and earth nature elements. As we integrate these energies, or Faeries, into our lives then we begin to find a balance and purpose in our lives. Each of us came into this life with a personal growth plan to allow our souls to evolve, but as lightworkers we also came with a global plan to allow us to help mother earth heal as she has been neglected and abused in the past.

Faeries are the beautiful and magical cousins of the Angels. We cannot work with Angels without working with Faeries. They are associated with nature and as such they have different elemental categories that they are associated with. The word fairy derives from the old French faerie which means "enchantment". These magnificent beings are the spirits of nature which dwell in every living thing upon the Earth. Faeries are the intrinsic inhabitants of nature and thus reflect the natural world in their appearance, culture and personality.

The Talmud states that "Every blade of grass has its angel that bends over it and whispers, "Grow, grow."" These Angels are the Faeries and they constantly work to aid wild animals and plants, protecting them and nurturing them as our Angels do us.

It has been my experience to use Angels to heal people emotionally, as many of our physical problems stem from long term emotional issues. I use the Elemental energies or Faeries to aid with healing physical ailments.

As we start to tune into nature, and leave our own egos behind we start to find that our lives and bodies start to follow that wonderful blueprint that was written many thousands to years before we were born. Below is a guide to the seasons and how they reflect and influence our lives.

Spring

In spring we start to plant new ideas and plan the next adventures that we will embark upon. This time is the start of manifestation. In spring our Angels start to nudge us to start new adventures, to "spring clean" our lives as well as our homes. This is because when we change nothing in our lives and continue day to day with the same energy, then as a spiritual being we become stagnant and cannot grow. However, when we change the energy around and within us with new activities and new inspiration through following the guidance of our Angels and the Angel within us then we allow ourselves to grow, as all of nature does in the spring. New shoots start to show and leaves appear on branches that are bare. The same is true of humans – as we allow that Angelic inspiration to guide us then our spiritual body starts to grown like a tree, opening and revealing it's true potential. This is the time of year that we can start to sow the seeds of what we want to manifest later in the year, so whether it is a new romance that you desire or a change in the direction of your career, then there is no better time to start it than now. When you go into the garden to plant the seeds of your favourite flowers that you wish to enjoy in the summer and autumn then take this time to communicate with the Faery energy that is ever present in nature and allow them to know what is in your heart. Plant a crystal in your garden as a symbol of your heart's desire and call upon Archangel Ariel to watch over the plant of your dreams and ask her to send the Faeries that she works with to aid in the manifestation.

Spring is represented by the Sylphs of the air that fly freely. Cousins to these beautiful Faeries are the wood sprites that are found in forests. Many people mistake butterflies and bumble bees for these beautiful airborne Faeries.

Summer

In summer we allow ourselves to watch our plans grow to fruition, and we allow ourselves to play in the sun. As a product of God the father and Gaia, Mother Earth, I always take time to be in tune with nature. When is the last time you watched the path of a bumble bee, saw how a red admiral butterfly is always attracted to dandelions first in the garden, or how even in the harshest environment a plant can still force through. Nature always finds a way. When we have all disappeared from this planet, nature will continue in some form or another. Take this time to allow yourself to bask in the energy that is all around you.

This is the time of years that the Devas are closest to us and I always sense and see their energy where there are foxgloves in the garden. They are like beautiful pillars of light in the garden and when I first started to "see" them I tried to pretend that really I was just seeing shafts of sunlight until one day they had decided that I had ignored them enough. The wind chimes hanging through the garden started to play a melody and as I stood there I heard a beautiful voice in my head that had the melody of the wind chimes say to me "we are the Devas, and we protect this sacred place". I was extremely shocked and yet so pleased at the same time that they had taken the time to communicate with someone as unimportant as myself.

It was at this point in my life that I started to see myself through the eyes of the different energies around me. My Angels, the Faeries, and the Devas did not see me as being unimportant – they saw me as an extension of them. I was here to help and work with these very special energies to give them a voice. At this time of year as we play, we start to notice all the different Faery energies around you. They are everywhere in nature and if you allow yourself the time to open your heart they are more that willing to work with the higher energy inside yourself – that Angel that resides inside you that is an extension of them and the nature that is all around you.

Summer is represented by the Salamanders of the fire element, and fire does not occur without these beautiful beings. These Faeries have no cousins and are in an exclusive group. Due to the nature of these energies caution and respect should always be used when working with them.

Autumn

In autumn we start to slow down and look back on all that we have achieved in the year, thankful for all our blessings and the harvest that life has provided for us. This is the time of year that Mother Nature sends her Faeries to start to put the plants and trees to sleep before winter sweeps the land. The goodness and life force of the flowers retreat back into the ground, the leaves start to fall off the trees and many animals stock pile food for their winter hibernation. This is a process that happens without us being aware of the subtle changes in our environment which herald in this new chapter in nature's life.

I often stand under a tree who is releasing it's leaves and release any cares or worries I have, knowing that this is an appropriate time and place to do so, in synchronicity with nature and it's guardians. My Mum used to tell me that the leaves were dancing in the wind with the Faeries as they fell to the ground. Nature has a unique ability to regenerate itself and this is seen every year when the trees lose their leaves. All the leaves fall from the trees, some are diseased and some are not, yet all come away. Nature at its most basic level knows that to survive it must remove that which no longer serves it – all that is diseased – so that the tree can survive.

I always like to look to nature to find solutions to what is going on in my life, and allow the seasons to guide me. This time of year as nature removes her summer clothes, is the most appropriate time of the year to remove any situation or person in your life that no longer serves your highest goals. Sometimes along the way it is hard as we have to let healthy aspects go, like the healthy leaves, in order to save what is precious to us. I have always found that when I follow my Angels inner guidance that if I release someone into the universe from my life, that if they are truly supposed to be in my life that my Guardian Angels catch them and send them back into it again. So never fear that you are releasing a person, place, or situation that is supposed to be in your life – it's not possible when you work with Angels.

The season of autumn is governed over by the water element of the Undines. The cousins to this group of Faeries are the water sprite, snow sprite, sea sprite, and Mermaids. These beings are very shy and you must be very patient if you want to see and work with them. I caught a beautiful sea sprite energy orb beside my beautiful dog

Oberon in a photograph. He is very much a little Faery and hence his name.

Winter

In winter we self reflect and allow our bodies to rest in preparation for the next phase of our lives. Sleep renews and reawakens passion in us. Do not be too rough on yourself during this season. At this time of year all the goodness has retreated into the earth and many of the Faeries that have been present all year round have followed the signs of nature and are in winter hibernation. The snow queen has swept across the land covering it with frost and snow, ensuring that all of nature is asleep.

My Angels always guide me at this time of year to follow nature and allow myself time to relax and breathe. This is the season that heralds in Christmas. At this time of year the earth's vibration changes as the Angelic choirs start to sing a different song of love. The Seraphim and Cherubim at the top of the choirs continually sing the praises of the creator to the created. However, at this time of the year their song changes in frequency, and we can feel its change reaching us here on the earth plane. This is also a special time of year in the calendar of Mother Earth. It symbolises one of the eight original festivals – that of winter solstice (also known as Yule or Midwinter). Having shed the leaves of the old year, from the 22nd December the days start to get longer, heralding in the New Year and all the spectacular splendour that Nature has to offer.

The earthly cousins of the Angels – the Faeries – also celebrate Christmas time, and the tradition of bringing a tree into the house at Winter Solstice was to ensure that the wood spirits had a place to shelter from the cold during this harshest part of winter time. Food and bells were hung on the tree so that the Faeries could eat, and also so that the people knew they were safely in their homes when they heard the bells ringing.

The season of winter is associated with the nature Faery of the Gnomes of the earth. The cousins of these hard working Faeries are the Elves, Brownies, and tree People (the dryads).

No matter whether you celebrate this time of year for the pagan festival of winter solstice or you celebrate the Christian festival of the birth of Christ, this is a special time of year for every plant, animal, or human on this planet. When all the shops finally close, and there is nothing else for us to do but stop and breathe we find that there is peace within us. That we no longer focus on the commercialisation of the season, but on what it actually means. It is a time when we actually send thoughts of love and light to our fellow man, and actually mean it.

At this time of year the Archangel who is closest to us and wants to work with us is Archangel Gabriel who wants to guide us to the end of the path that we are currently on as this year ends, and into our true life purpose as we start a New Year with our Angels. Archangel Gabriel is the Archangel who governs over communication. Therefore we should surround ourselves with the beautiful copper energy of Archangel Gabriel at this time of the year and allow ourselves to communicate with one another, with ourselves in honesty and love, and most especially with our own Guardian Angels who are there guiding and guarding us every day of our lives – take time out this festive time to allow yourselves a little me time with your Angels.

Working with Nature Energies.

Each season has an Archangel and Faery element associated with it:

The compass of Life:

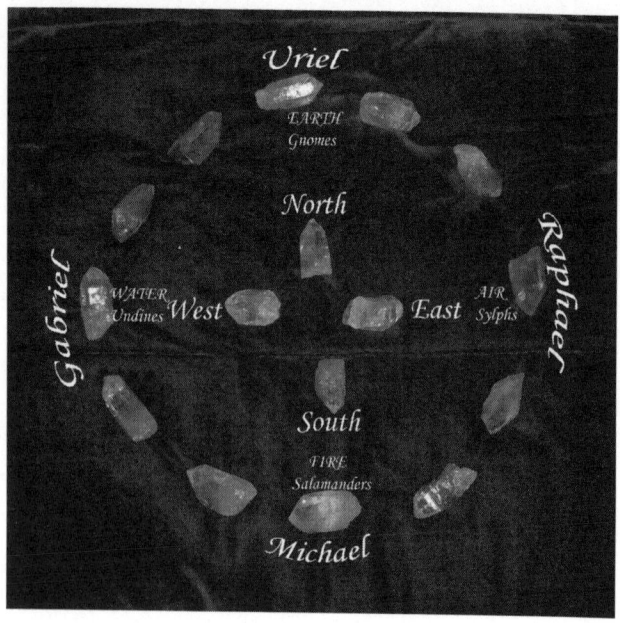

I find that in working with the Angelic energies you cannot help but work with the energies of nature. After all the Faeries are the cousins of the Angels. When you consider the spiritual realms they are in essence energy levels. At the top of this is the nine choirs of Angels, followed by the Faery realms, and then by the hierarchy of spirit. The densest energy being ourselves incarnated here on the earth plane.

Nine Choirs of Angels

Seraphim
Cherubim
Thrones
Dominions
Virtues
Powers
Principalities
Archangels
Angels

Faery Realms

Devas
Faery Kings / Queens
Fae
Elemental / nature spirits

Spirit Realms

Cosmic Guides
Ascended Masters
Spirit Guides
– Human / animal form
Loved ones

Over the years I have caught some very interesting pictures with lights and figures in them that I attribute to Faery energy. I would advise that anyone wishing to work with Faery energies start with the Sylphs of the air, as these energies are the boldest of the Faeries in my experience and respond well to working with humans. Go into nature and start to visualise them in your mind's third eye. Start to picture the colour of their hair, their skin tone, what their wings look like. Imagine them as they blow playfully in the wind. How do you visualise these beautiful spirits of nature? I would often sit in front of foxgloves as these are a particular favourite of the Sylphs. If you train your physical eyes to look just beyond the flower and allow your eyes to defocus slightly then you will start to see flashes of light around the flowers – this is the Faerie energy.

As your relationship progresses start to bring the Faeries gifts – such as chocolate, milk, or a small crystal. Do not be alarmed if the chocolate is still there the next day. Faeries are beings of energy. They will not eat the food but will merely take the goodness out of it. They will be grateful for the gesture. The milk goes into the ground as an offering to Mother Earth in acknowledgement that the Faeries are her children – the energy of the milk will nourish them. Organic milk is preferable, but they won't mind what type you give them. Some of my student's give the Faeries in their gardens chocolate milk with wonderful results!

You will find that you start to feel compelled into environmental issues, such as recycling, collecting rubbish that other thoughtless individuals have left behind, or helping animals. All of these are positive signs that you are working with nature energies. They may not be able to collect the bags on the beach that can harm the marine animals, but they can urge willing hands of their human friends to do it for them.

One of my favourite gifts for the Faeries is a small rose quartz crystal. It does not matter what type the crystal is, rose quartz is merely my personal preference. I will put it in the ground, into a tree stump, a body of water, or wherever my Angel within guides me to. I always tell the Faeries either telepathically or vocally that this gift is for them and that they are to use the energy of the crystal for the highest good of Mother Earth. My Faery guides joke with me quite often that they can track where I have been on the earth by the trail of rose quartz hearts with my love on them.

Finally, when you feel that your relationship is in a place of trust and mutual respect, you can take your camera along and ask their permission to take a few pictures and have a look at the results!

This photograph was taken at Shane's Castle on the day of Summer Solstice. I was walking through an old graveyard when a flash of light at my eyes made me step back. When I took a photograph, this naughty Faery was flying away from me.

This photograph was taken at Cairn wood while I was walking my dogs. I was taking photographs of the woods that we were walking through, and caught this little Faery on film.

Auric Exercises

This section of the book has gentle exercises that you can practice on yourself and with others to increase your psychic abilities that will in turn help to increase your faith and trust in your own abilities and advice.

Exercises to improve your connection to your Angel Within and the higher realms

I have found that the constant opinion is that because I take Angel workshops then I am expected to constantly see 6ft Angels with every class member, be in constant contact with the spirit realm and have an active relationship with Faeries. Nothing could be further from the truth. I am just like you. I go to work, do the shopping, and do all the normal tasks that everyone else does. The only difference is that I am in constant contact with my Guardian Angels and the Angel within myself. I LISTEN to their advice and I ACT on it. I ask for help and direct action. The most profound piece of advice that I was ever given along my life's journey was to look at the letters in the word Angel.

It starts with   **A**sk
                              N
                              G
                              E
And ends in   **L**isten

So when you start to "ask" for angelic intervention, make sure that you "listen" for the answer. If that inner voice tells me to take a turn off to the right as I'm driving along and trying to find someone's house for a reading, even if the map tells me to go straight ahead, I will turn my car right. I can be assured that 100% of the time that there is either something that my Angels require me to see, or there is a problem with the road ahead and they are detouring me to the destination. I want to point out at this point that although Angels do not require you to thank them, unlike Faeries, I personally always feel that if it is worth asking for, it is worth being thankful for. When we work with Angels one thought plays through my head when I invoke Angels to help me – I may not always get what I want, but I always get what I need. It is so true that when I look back over my life that I thank God and the Angels for unanswered prayers. It's not that they ignored me, but merely postponed their reply until I was in the right place to hear them. Once again reinforcing the "ask and listen" philosophy. I feel compelled to share a story with you about asking your Angels for help and guidance and then listening for their reply. When I say listen, it is not merely our Clairaudience we use when we are listening for our Angels reply – it is all our Clairs as we are a spiritual whole when we use all of them together. I had been taking an Angel class one Thursday night when my Mum, my brother Simon and I returned home. My Dad met us at the door with the news that one of my chinchillas (Chelsea) had had a baby. All our cages were made so that if a female gave birth that the male could be segregated to the top part of the cage to give Mummy and baby time together for the first week or two after she gave birth. Dad told Mum and I that he had put Apollo (the daddy) up in the top part of the cage. This cage reached about 8 feet in the air and to access the top part for cleaning and feeding etc I need to use a step ladder. I could not understand why our Chelsea did not bond with the baby. She was always sitting on the top shelf of her three tier cage where it joined the top section where Apollo was. She had not fed baby Star and it was getting to the three day point that if the baby was not fed it would die. I had been feeding it baby milk – but that was not the same as his mother's milk. On the Saturday night I stood with my right hand to the top of the cage where Chelsea was and my left hand down where baby Star was and I said these words:

"Angels I ask that you reconnect that which has been disconnected"

Now, in my mind I meant Chelsea and baby Star – as I had left the statement so open my Angels had other ideas. In the three days since the birth my Dad had been cleaning Apollo's cage and feeding him. That night as I stood vigil on Star I noticed that Apollo wasn't coming to the front of the cage for his favourite treat of cabbage. I started to feel very uneasy and so I climbed the stepladders to the cage to lift him out and make sure he was OK. When I got there I was shocked and surprised to find two other baby chinchillas who had not been with their mother from when they were born three days previously. Chelsea had not been a bad mother; she had desperately been trying to get to her other babies that she was separated from. Mum and I spent the next few weeks feeding the babies with milk every 2-3 hours. They all survived and I am very glad to say still with us today. This story shows that our Angels can answer our prayers through feelings and that once again I may not have gotten what I want, but I got what I needed.

Feeling the Aura

Notice how I did not use the words feeling the "human" aura. Every living being on this planet has a living aura – an energy field that surrounds it that we can feel physically and emotionally at all times. When we move into the world of spirit we still have an energy field, but that becomes known as our "spirit" or sometimes our "soul". Clients have told me repeatedly that they can feel their loved ones that have passed over – Clairsentience (or clear feeling) works through sensing a change in the pressure around your body. I normally feel this as tingling on certain areas of my body depending on what energy I am working with. It can also be experienced through smelling a scent unexpectedly. The third way is for you to experience a taste, again depending on the energy you are working with. Every energy that you experience is different and eventually you can start to discern individual energies. How many times have you known who is standing behind you before you have turned around?

To start to work as a spiritual being I have found in the classes that I teach that when people start to feel energies physically with their hands they progress in leaps and bounds in their psychic work. This is because their ego can no longer tell them that what they feel is their imagination. Suddenly the whole world of energy becomes very real. I selected the name for the people we trained as "Angel Energists". This was due to the fact that I insist that as a being of spirit we must be able to work with all energies – the Angels in the heavens, the Faeries of the Earth, and the Spirits and Spirit Animals of the lower world. When they can work with these energies completely and interchangeable I am happy that they are certified to work as Angel Energists.

The first exercise that I teach is how to feel your own Aura – after all, how can we expect to feel other beings Auras if we cannot feel our own? Find a partner that you can work with and place your hands in the prayer position in front of you. Your partner will place their hands over yours and apply a slight pressure as you try to pull your hands apart. After about 90 seconds your partner removes their hands and you spread your hands out as far as they will go. Now start to bring them together again slowly with your eyes closed. When you feel a slight resistance - stop. This is where you will have a width of your Aura in your hands. This is the physical layer of your Aura, and it is the first layer of your Aura that surrounds your body.

Repeat this several times and you will increase your confidence and will be able to start to feel your own Aura at will without applying the pressure first. It is all about practice.

For those people reading this who do not have someone they can call upon to be their spiritual partner for these exercises then I have included a how to do these exercises on your own. I appreciate that not everyone is out of the spiritual closet and that's fine as we have all hid in there at some point in our lives. When you feel safe to step out of it, know that your Angels will be there to guide your first steps to you finding likeminded people – our soul mates – who will help us along our climb up the spiritual ladder. I thank God and the Angels everyday that they provided me with these wonderful people in my family, so that I could flourish under their love and guidance and feel safe to talk about Angels from a very early age.

The solo exercise is very easy. Adopt the prayer position with your hands while sitting. Place your hands between your knees and allow your knees to be the pressure that the extra set of hands would have provided. The rest is the same.

****

The next exercise that I get my class members to participate in is using their ability to feel the Aura to start to feel Chakra areas. We have seven major chakras that run up our body in line with our spines and our central nervous system. I would suggest that you pick one of these Chakras (such as the solar plexus) and a minor Chakra such as those found on your elbow or knee. Again you can do this with a partner or by yourself. Rub your hands together to activate your hand Chakras. Use your receiving hand – the one that you do NOT write with – and close your eyes and if you are working with a partner ask them to close their eyes too. Removing the physical eyes allows you to work more closely with your psychic senses. Then hold your receiving hand about six inches over a major Chakra, for example the solar plexus found at the belly button region. Allow yourself to visualise this energy point through your psychic senses – feel the energy through your hands, visualise the colour and the brightness of the colour that you sense through your receiving hand. Now feel a minor Chakra through your receiving hand allowing yourself to sense the energy and visualise any colours you receive in connection with this Chakra. Compare the energy that you felt between these two energy centres. Every Chakra has a different energy as they rotate at different speeds and the speed that they rotate at relates to the colour associated with them. Note all your findings in your Angel diary as you sense and feel different Chakras.

****

Allow yourself the time to master these first two techniques. As you read through them you will think they are very simple and that you may not need to spend long on each of them. You must remember that working in the Spiritual field takes time and that if a skill is worth having, it is worth the time to learn. I would advise people to spend at least a month using each of these techniques until they become second nature to you and that you start to communicate with your Angel within as you use them. You will start to find that you will receive information about people as you sense their Aura and their Chakras. It is when you start to receive this information and process it through the Angel found within yourself that you will be ready to move onto the next technique.

****

There are many hundreds of minor Chakras on your hands and feet that allow us to ground ourselves through our feet and allow us to feel and express ourselves through our hands. It is no mistake that many of the Lightworkers found on the planet today are sensitive, expressive people who use their hands to aid them when they communicate. I find it very difficult to talk or to teach and not use my hands. One night as I took one of my awareness classes I made a conscious decision to stop using my hands while I talked. I found that where normally I would never have to use notes as I communicate directly from the Angels, I started to become distracted and lost track of what I was saying. However, when I started using my hands again the energy and creativity that is me came back into focus. I have noticed this quite frequently in people that I work with. I believe this is to do with the fact that we use our hands as antennae picking up information and also sending it out to the people that we talk to. People remember more about what a person who "talks with their hands" says as they hear it twice – once through their ears and once through their psychic senses. Therefore never underestimate the power that you hold in your hands and the intent that they represent.

In the previous technique you used your hands to sense the difference in the energy between the different

Chakras in the body, and we also learnt the sensation of feeling the Aura. We are now going to meld these techniques together to form a useful technique that is powerful and healing. We are going to learn how to sense imbalances in the Chakras through the Aura.

Work with a partner – a Spiritual buddy that you trust to work with. Ask them to stand with their arms by their sides and close their eyes. You are going to stand to one side of them. Activate your hand Chakras by rubbing your hands together. Now starting at their root Chakra, place one hand in front of your partners root Chakra and one hand behind. This forms a giving and receiving energy loop that the Chakra is inside. Your giving hand is the hand that you write with, while your receiving hand is the hand that you do not write with. By placing your hands a few inches out from the person's body you are still in the first layer of their Aura but are not physically touching them. It is all about energy. As they have their eyes closed they will not know which Chakra you are working on and cannot put up any barriers or prejudices, thus changing the information you receive. You will notice that their body will do one of three things unconsciously.

1) It will stay still, perfectly balanced between your two hands. This will tell you that the Chakra is energetically balanced.
2) It will sway towards your giving hand. This will show you that this Chakra is in need of energy and is swaying towards this hand to gain energy as this is your energetic giving hand.

3) Their body will sway away from your giving hand and towards your receiving hand. This will let you know that there is too much energy in this Chakra and that it is shying away from your giving hand, but also moving towards your receiving hand as it is trying to remove excess energy by giving it to you.

Move to the sacral Chakra, then the solar plexus Chakra, the heart Chakra, the throat Chakra, the third eye Chakra, and lastly the crown Chakra. Share with your partner the energetic information you received from their Chakras and allow them to share with you what they experienced throughout the exercise.

The fact that the body is like a pendulum moving through its crystalline matrixes allows for imbalances to show in this way. Your body will move like a pendulum if you ask it "yes" and "no" questions. It is a fun technique to learn, but ultimately you cannot go around with a pendulum in your hand, or your body swaying in everyday life. These are techniques used to confirm what we have communicated between our conscious minds and the Angelic advice that resides inside us.

****

Again allow yourself adequate time to learn this technique. Once these techniques are learnt properly they will be inbuilt inside you and you will start to use them as part of yourself without questioning or thinking.

The last part of this section puts all that we have

learnt together and allows us to balance Chakras with our hands, to help and aid our friends and family. We must remember that imbalances or blockages in the energy network that is our Chakra system can result in an adverse manifestation in our physical, emotional, spiritual, or mental health. The four components that make up the four layers of our Aura.

Check your partner's Chakra to see if they are in balance or not. Now that you know the energetic flow of the person's Chakras we once again start with the root Chakra. It does not matter what size a person's Chakras are as long as they are all the same size. Visualise a beautiful ball of vibrant red energy that is the root Chakra. See the person's Chakra energy being cleansed and purified, all negativity being removed. Allow yourself to sense any information that the Chakra wishes to share with you. This may be information about what has caused the imbalance or why it has become shrunken or swollen in size. When a Chakra is smaller in size than it should be it is due to a person, place, or situation worrying the person. A Chakra which is swollen or larger in size than it should be shows that a person is obsessing about a person, place, or situation relating to that Chakra. The root Chakra is affected by issues related to sex, money, and material needs.

We then move to the sacral Chakra and visualise a ball of beautiful bright orange light the same size as the red ball of light that represents the root Chakra. See and sense the sacral Chakra being cleansed, allowing all negativity to be purified and removed from the person. Allow any information from the sacral Chakra to be communicated to you regarding inner child issues, physical desires, and addictions.

The solar plexus Chakra governs over survival issues, power, and control. As you visualise a ball of bright, beautiful yellow energy the same size as the first two Chakras, sense the solar plexus Chakra being purified, all negativity washed away out of their lives. Communicate with the solar plexus Chakra and find the truth behind why it was imbalanced.

Once we finish balancing the lower level Chakras governing over earthly concerns and issues we move into the higher level Chakras which govern over Spiritual development.

The emotional heart is the centre of our seven Chakra system. The heart Chakra is a beautiful emerald green colour and is the energy centre which allows Clairsentience to develop and grow inside us. It is the ability that allows us to sense and feel energies and is the most sensitive of the four Clairs that we work with as a Spiritual being. As you connect to the person's heart Chakra envisage a ball of healing green light the same size as you have visualised the previous Chakras. Allow healing energy to flow in the heart centre, cleansing it of heartache and betrayal. Feel as the negative is replaced by the positive, healing the person in all directions of time and space.

Moving to the throat Chakra we allow ourselves to help release any blockages towards our partner speaking their Spiritual truth and creativity. We visualise the throat Chakra as a ball of brilliant blue energy. Allow all fears and negativity surrounding speaking their truth to be cleansed away, releasing any resentment towards those who can and do speak their spiritual truth. Let creative energy flow back into their throat Chakra, balancing it to be the same size as the other Chakras you have already worked on.

The third eye Chakra is connected to psychic abilities and Spiritual sight. It governs over Clairvoyance which is the Spiritual gift that people want in their lives. The greatest fear that holds a Spiritual being from fulfilling their potential and moving onto Spiritual enlightenment is the fear of seeing. People always tell me how they want to see Angels or departed loved ones. On a few occasions these people have been granted their wish and they become frightened and declare that they no longer want to see. This is the fear based response that stops us from truly seeing. As you balanced this Chakra remember this and as you pour empowering indigo energy in send healing to this energy centre as well, allowing the person to Spiritually see what they can cope with at this point in their life. Never try to open someone's Spiritual sight more than their Angels want at any time, after all the Angels know what is right for their charge. Open their Spiritual sight to the truth within them, so that they can see their true potential and the light that is within them. Allow them to see the blessings in their lives and how to use them fully for their life purpose.

The last Chakra in this system is the crown

Chakra and it governs over Spiritual development and Claircognizance. The colour associated with this Chakra is a vibrant violet colour with sparkles of white running through it. Balance this Chakra with the same size ball of violet light as you used for the other coloured Chakras. Send healing and love into this energy centre and allow it to connect all the other Chakras in their system. As you communicate with this last Chakra communicate with the person as a whole Spiritual being. Allow the essence of their complete psychic being to meld together for them to connect as one. We sometimes disjoint ourselves and separate ourselves into different parts which represent different aspects, instead of being one functioning soul.

I always ask that a Chakra balance is sealed with the violet flame so that the person is spiritually and psychically protected.

Share with your partner all that you have learned for them through this session. You will find that as you practice this technique its strength will grow within you and you will find that although it is simple it is also one of the most healing tools you will attach to your Spiritual tool belt.

Meditations

In this section of the book I wish to share with you some of the meditations I have used personally and also with my Angel Energist practitioner classes with great success and insight. You can read through these mediations and then put on some gently music and follow the general trend of the meditation, or you can record it and play it back to yourself. It is all down to personal choice and how you feel about listening to your own voice, which some people can find very distracting.

Think of meditation as a beautiful gift that you are giving to yourself to connect with your Guardian Angels and the wonderful Angel within yourself. Practicing meditation regularly with breath and intention can transform your life by renewing your soul and spirit, which in turn gives us health in our body and mind. In this section we learn to silence our lower mind that tells us we have better things to be doing with our time that meditate – such as shopping, cleaning, cooking etc. Allow your lower mind to read through all its lists and then allow your higher mind to start to visualise through your imagination the meditations that are in this section. You can simply read a paragraph and then visualise it, until in the end you will be able to enjoy the full meditation and the great gifts that it brings to you. Enjoy this time, in perfect knowledge that you are gaining great gifts, a closer relationship with the Angels, and a stillness of mind that will allow you to hear the inner guidance that will guide your life into where you want to take it.

Meet your Guardian Angel Meditation

Put your feet on the ground to Mother Earth, and point your head to God. Breathe in and out deeply, letting go of all the worries of today. As you breathe, imagine roots growing up from the earth and covering your feet. You will feel beautiful green energy from mother earth moving up from your feet, up your legs, through your Root Chakra at the bottom of your spine, through your Sacral Chakra, and up through your Solar Plexus Chakra to your Heart Chakra; where it mingles with the green energy that is your Heart Chakra.

Now feel a golden white energy coming from the sky and in through your Crown Chakra, down through your Third Eye Chakra, and your Throat Chakra, and let this energy meet and mingle with the green energy in your Heart Chakra.

Where these energies meet is where you are going to meet your Guardian Angels. Now, as you breathe focus on the pause between the in and the out breath. As you do this you will see a path which leads into a forest. I want you to start to travel down this path now. You are travelling down and as you do you are aware of a river running alongside the path. I want you in your own time to go and stand in the river. The water is warm and when you look down it is filled with different coloured crystals. You reach down and pick up a crystal. This is a gift for you from you Angels, and they want you to keep this crystal inside your heart area where it will help you to heal your heart from hurt, disappointment, grief, anger, loss, and pain.

As you emerge on the other side of the river you are aware that you are again walking down a path through the forest. As you are walking down the path you are aware that you are coming to a clearing. As you walk into the clearing I want you to look around you and take in all the wonders surrounding you. This is where the faeries live. They are flitting around you and playing through the flowers and the trees. You can see water sylphs playing in the river, look over to your left, because in between the trees if you look really carefully – you will see a unicorn. She is truly beautiful and has magical energy surrounding her everywhere. The faeries are flitting around her and moving her mane like the wind. Take you time to look around, and breathe in the Faery energy – enjoy the Faery energy.

When you are ready look up and see a path leading up a hillside, and there on the trail beckoning you is Archangel Michael. Follow him and he will lead you to a structure. It will take on whatever form you wish it to. It could be a temple, or a hut, or a house, or a roman column structure. The door to this structure will be open or the flowing curtain will bellow out to form an opening. Archangel Michael will show you inside.

Take a really good look at the way that the room inside is furnished. What colours do you see around you? These are the colours that are in your physical aura at this time in your life. There is a table in the room and you will see chairs around it. You go and sit at the table, and when you are comfortable you look over to the door and Archangel Michael shows in your Guardian Angels. They are beings of pure love and light and they come across the room and join you at the table. Archangel Michael closes the door and stands outside like a bouncer who will not let negative energies in.

Your Guardian Angels have left gifts on the table for you. These are uniquely for you, and I ask you to lift them and have a look, as you will receive conformation of these in the physical world within the next few days. Now is the time for you to ask your Guardian Angels anything you wish, even if it is simply "What do I need to know today". Or you could just sit in their energy for a few minutes – it's up to you.

Now you see Archangel Michael opening the door and beckoning you to join him. You say good-bye to your Angels, and join Archangel Michael at the door – don't forget to give Michael a BIG HUG. You once again travel along the path – this time away from the structure and to the clearing. Have a look around to see if there are any different energies there – if there are, these could be energies that your Angels wish you to start working with.

When you are ready you continue down the path, across the river and back to the start of your journey.

Once again become conscious of your breathing, and as you do bring yourself back to consciousness, wiggling your fingers and toes; and when you're ready – opening your eyes.

Secret Garden Meditation

As the music enfolds you, you are already beginning to relax and let go of any stress, tension, or worry. Exhale anything that could be on your mind; that you would like to release.

I want you to envisage that you are standing beside a door and to the right of the door there is three keys, each a different colour. There is Copper for Archangel Gabrielle, there is Light Pink for the Archangel Ariel, and there is Violet for Archangel Jeremiel. You chose whatever key suits you at this time and open the door. As you enter this secret garden, you will be aware of beautiful colours and butterfly-like creatures swooping around you. There is a pathway in front of you and as you look you can see that it is a chakra pathway.

The first flowers you walk through on the path are red roses – you stop to smell them and they have a beautiful scent and red admiral butterflies playing on them. The next flowers are orange tiger-lilies and they have tiny butterflies called small coppers flying around, playing through them. The bright yellow, beautiful sunflowers have bumble bees merrily collecting their sweet nectar and busily buzzing through them. Next is the herb garden of lush green foliage, which has green caterpillars munching away on them. This green is the heart of the path and nurtures the caterpillars into beautiful butterflies. The blue Irises stand proud as the throat chakra of the garden, and peeking out from among them are the cheeky little blue tits that are playing hide-and-seek. The Indigo pansies are delicate and fragile and are cared for by the nature spirits – they are the representation of our third eye chakra; and finally as you walk through the violet violas, feel the connection to your higher self – the part of you that is 100% psychic and happy to be so. Embrace your higher self and feel the power of your psychic self; feel how right it is to be psychic and allow yourself to be 100% psychic once more.

Now you are in the garden proper, and you can see that the path ran down the middle of a perfect circle. In front of you is a semicircle of foxgloves. I want you to spend a few moments looking at the foxgloves and watching the faeries playing in them. Notice what they look like to you. Enjoy the playfulness of them, and listen to what they have to tell you.

As you turn to your left there is a patch of bright yellow primroses. They are all planted in rows and look like rows of houses, because that is exactly what they are – they are homes for gnomes. If you look very carefully you can see little gnomes moving between them, and some of them are lying in the primroses sleeping in the sun. Look at their appearance; sense the emotions they give to you.

At the back of the left hand side of the garden there is a clump of mighty oak trees growing. And beside them several pink roses which are in bloom. I would invite you to pick seven petals of the roses and sprinkle them around one of the oak trees, to see what happens.

You will start to see the wood nymphs playing through the oaks. They have beautiful autumnal colours and copper red wings, with a flowing green dress. Listen to their voices; hear what they have to say, and what travels to you on the wind. They are a beautiful group of nature spirits and have inspirational messages for all of us.

You walk back up through the garden, back to the foxglove haven and you start to travel down the other side of the garden. On this side there runs a trickling river, which tumbles over stones. There are leaves floating along the river, and if you look carefully you can see water nymphs riding on them.

Also, swimming through the river playing with the fish are the water undines – they have tails instead of legs and very pale bodies, with long flowing hair. I ask that you sit beside this peaceful river for a few moments to communicate with both of these types of nature spirit. Ask them about their life in the water, and what messages they have for you.

We now travel to the back of the garden and here there is a beautiful waterfall. The water nymphs also play here, but this is a sacred place – because here there is a powerful goddess energy and it is here we can look into the waterfall mirror to see our true form. I want you to approach this place with reverence and walk into the water

– stand in this water for a few moments to connect with this magical energy. Then when you are ready, I want you to open your third eye and look into the waterfall. The water is moving so quickly that it has formed a mirror, and as you look into the mirror what do you see?

Do you have the eagle wings of an Angel?

Do you have the dragonfly Faery wings of the elemental kingdom?

Are you wearing a beautiful flowing priestess/sorceress gown depicting your connection with ancient lifetimes as a healer or priestess?

Spend a few minutes looking at your true self. As you do so you can ask yourself questions, to get to know the true essence of you a little bit better. And women while you are there – reconnect with your inner goddess and men reconnect with your feminine side. Ask your higher self what you spiritual gifts are?

While you are standing there looking at yourself spiritually you realise that the waterfall is opening and forming a doorway, and you walk inside. You find yourself inside a crystal geode and waiting for you is a Faery guide to help you connect with nature on a daily basis. You feel a link moving between your heart and the heart of your Faery guide. Accept their energy as part of your own and allow them to reconnect with you fully, mingling your energy and theirs. Allow yourself to sit comfortably in this energy for a few moments as you connect with them, knowing that when you leave this special place you bring this guide with you.

Speak to your guide and introduce yourself. Learn a little more about them. Let them know about you. Ask what gifts do they bring into your life?

It is now time for us to leave this crystal geode and this garden of our heart, and as we travel back up the garden towards the foxgloves a white hare is sitting in the garden in front of us, and as we look at it; it transforms into a Faery queen. She has beautiful flowing white hair and a purple flowing gown. She smiles at you, winks and turns back into a hare and runs off into the foxgloves.

You walk back up the pathway towards the door, and as you approach it the door magically opens for you to leave. Bring yourself back into consciousness of your present body, and allow yourself to remember your time with the faeries. Gently and easily begin to move your body and breathe out any feelings of sadness you have about leaving the faeries. Remembering only the joy and the love, letting everything else go. Keeping your magical power of spiritual sight awakened and fully alive. Know it is safe for you to be powerful. Know that it is safe for you to fully commit yourself to your divine purpose in life. Know that the Faeries and their love are always with you and in your heart.

The Rainbow of Angels Meditation

Rainbows have been a sign of hope and promise throughout every culture on the earth. The rainbow is an ancient and universal symbol, which often represents the connection between human beings on earth and God. A rainbow was reported in the Bible (Genesis 9:13) when the rescued on Noah's ark watched the first rainbow at the end of the Flood, which God sent as a symbol that they would never have to suffer a flood like that again. In Greek mythology it was associated with the goddess Iris, who brought messages from the gods on Mount Olympus. She was often seen flying from earth to heaven creating a rainbow bridge behind her.

In nature the highest most bow of the Rainbow is the colour red, but humans are a mirror image of nature and therefore red represents our bottom charka, the root charka. We work from the densest colour of red through to the spiritual colour of enlightenment violet. This meditation allows you to connect to your Soul Guardian Angel and your Life Purpose Guardian Angel through the arch of Rainbow love. It also clears your charkas safely and peacefully, moving blockages and replacing the negativity that you have removed with positive new energy to allow you to move on in your life.

I want you to find somewhere comfortable, you can sit down or lie down, but ensure that you are comfortable and your body will not disturb you from your time of peace. Start to breathe – breathing in for four and out for four, regulating your breathing. Breathe in for four and tense all your muscles, now relax them again and breathe out. Do this several times until you feel your body's muscles relaxing completely. As your body relaxes you become aware of an Angel on each side of you. These are the two Guardian Angels that have guided you through your entire life. You are completely safe and at peace with them. They are loving guides and guardians who you trust completely and who surround you in a beautiful bright sparkling white light. You let this light surround you and you start to breathe it in.

You are completely surrounded and filled with the light and love of your Guardian Angels. Take a moment in their presence and allow yourself to communicate with them. Ask them the important question of What do I need to know today? Give your worries to your Angels. Allow them to take them away for transmutation through light and love to be used for the highest good in the universe.

As you are in this blissful state of oneness with your Guardian Angels you become aware that a beautiful rainbow has started to come out of the ground beside you. It arches up through your Soul Guardian Angel at your side and starts to flow through you – its red bow flowing through your root charka, its orange bow through your sacral charka, the yellow bow through your solar plexus charka. The green bow flows through your beautiful heart charka, the blue bow through you throat charka, the indigo bow through your third-eye charka. Finally the beautiful vibrant violet bow flows through your crown charka. This complete rainbow flows through your Life-purpose Guardian Angel standing at the other side of you and back down into Mother Earth.

The first bow that you become aware of is the red bow flowing through your root charka. The energy flows up from Mother Earth bringing life giving energy to you, infused with love by your Soul Guardian Angel. All the old and negative energy that has clouded your root charka starts to move out of your body and is transmuted through your Life-purpose Guardian Angel and planted into Mother Earth as beautiful seeds of love that will blossom into opportunities in the physical world. Let go of all issues relating to sex, money, and material needs in your life. Letting them all flow out of you in an act of releasement in exchange for peace and harmony in your life.

The second bow of the energy rainbow is the orange bow. It arches up from the earth, through your Soul Guardian Angel bringing beautiful vibrant energy into your body and into your sacral Chakra. This Chakra relates to inner child issues, physical desires, and addiction in your life. All the stale energy that is in your sacral Chakra starts to move out as it is replaced by this new energy that is flowing into you. The old energy moves out of you body and is transmuted through love and light by your Life-purpose Guardian Angel. This energy is sent into the universe as a beautiful bouquet of flowers and love.

The third bow of the rainbow is the yellow bow, which arches up from Mother Earth, through your Soul Guardian Angel allowing the beautiful vibrant energy to flow into your solar plexus Chakra. This Chakra governs over survival issues in your life, and issues concerning power and control in your life. As this new energy starts to move and flow through your solar plexus Chakra the old energy begins to move out from your body into you Life-purpose Guardian Angel for transmutation, and returned to Mother Earth to bring healing energy into her soil.

The fourth bow of the rainbow arches up from the ground and through your Soul Guardian Angel. This loving, healing green energy flows into your heart Chakra bringing emotional healing into your heart. Allow images to float into your mind, showing you the people, places, and situations that have hurt you greatly in the past and also in the present time. As these images come to mind allow the vibrant green energy to bathe them, surrounding them with healing light as they flow into your Life-purpose Guardian Angel for transmutation. Allow yourself the time to clear your heart Chakra of negativity as this Chakra governs over Clairsentience which is the most sensitive of all the psychic gifts that we use. As we cleanse this Chakra we will begin to find our own sensitivity increasing and clearing. You will start to feel the flow of energy that is moving through your heart Chakra slowing as the Chakra is fully cleansed and restored.

The fifth bow of the rainbow emerges from the ground and arches up through your Soul Guardian Angel and into your throat Chakra, which governs over spiritual truth and creativity. As the blue energy flows into your throat Chakra you will start to feel the dense energy that has formed when you have suppressed your spiritual truth over the years start to move as new vibrant blue energy starts to flow into the Chakra, cleansing and releasing all the old energy and old patterns; allowing them to flow into your Life-purpose Guardian Angel for transmutation and healing, sending it into Mother Earth.

The sixth indigo bow of the rainbow comes up through Mother Earth and arches up through your Soul Guardian Angel and into your third eye Chakra. This Chakra aids you with you psychic abilities. As your awareness is taken to this Chakra you become aware of the fog that is surrounding and filling this Chakra, a fog that means you cannot clearly see psychically. As the new energy from the rainbow flows through this Chakra you start to see beautiful indigo and white sparkling lights in the area of your third eye Chakra. The old energy of fear and regret starts to flow out of this Chakra and into your Life-purpose Guardian Angel for transmutation, love, and healing so that you can move on in your life and psychic development.

The seventh and final bow of this magical rainbow comes out of Mother Earth and arches up through your Soul Guardian Angel and into your crown Chakra and over into your Life-purpose Guardian Angel before re-entering Mother Earth and completing the rainbow that flows through you. The crown Chakra governs over spiritual enlightenment and your link to the Angelic realms. Healing violet energy enters this Chakra and purifies it, igniting the energy of the violet flame to protect and guide you.

Your Guardian Angels come to stand one in front and one behind you sealing the energy of the rainbow into your Chakras and as they do this you once again become aware of the room that you are sitting it, and they come to stand behind you as you wiggle your fingers and toes and slowly open your eyes.

The Vortex of the Archangels

The Archangels that are the best known and used by humans serve on the seven rays of spiritual enlightenment. This meditation introduces us to these magnificent beings and allows us to connect with their energy for us to work with them.

Find yourself a comfortable place for a little time of spiritual selfishness. A time dedicated to you to experience the energy of the seven rays of enlightenment and the Archangels associated with them. Start to control your breathing and relax each muscle in your body, starting with your feet and working your way up to the top of your head. Tensing and relaxing each muscle system until you are completely relaxed and comfortable.

When you are in a state of relaxed consciousness you become aware of beautiful sparkling white lights surrounding you. They swirl around you forming a beautiful vortex of light energy around you. White is the colour of your Guardian Angels. Know that when you are in this energy vortex they are constantly protecting their charges and keeping them safe and secure in their arms. As you stand in the middle of this vortex you become aware of different colours swirling past you.

The first colour you become aware of is a beautiful blue. This first ray is associated with Archangel Michael and it is the ray of faith, protection, and power. As this blue ray surrounds you breathe in its colour and feel the energy of Archangel Michael as he surrounds you. This ray provides us with physical and spiritual protection. Allow the energy and power of this ray to instil a pure and steadfast faith in yourself and in your belief in Angels. Archangel Michael will aid you onto your Life Purposes pathway – feel his energy as he shares with you what you were sent here to do in this lifetime. Know that Archangel Michael is only a call away when you need him in your everyday life. As you breathe deeply the blue light returns to the vortex as it continues to swirl around you, sparkling white light with colours intermingled.

The second colour you become aware of is a vibrant yellow colour. The second ray is associated with Archangel Jophiel and it is the ray of illumination and wisdom. As the yellow ray surrounds your physical body you breathe in the colour and feel the energy of Archangel Jophiel as she surrounds and comforts you. Align yourself with this ray as it introduces inspiration, understanding, and deep wisdom into your life. Archangel Jophiel will shine illumination on a situation that concerns you in your life at this time. Know that she will help you heal this situation and bring greater clarity into your life. As you breathe the yellow light returns to the vortex, which continues to swirl around you.

The third colour your attention is drawn to is passionate pink. The third ray is associated with Archangel Chamuel and is the ray of love and gratitude. As this wonderful pink ray surrounds you and you breathe it in you feel the calm and loving energy of Archangel Chamuel as he sends love to all four layers of your Aura into your physical body. This unconditional divine love permeates into your body and infuses into all your organs. Archangel Chamuel gives you help and guidance in all matters of the heart and compassion. Allow Archangel Chamuel to let you see the beauty within yourself and start to love yourself as a beautiful creation of God. Send this loving healing energy to loved ones and allow any divisions between family and friends to be healed through divine love. As you breathe the pink light returns to the vortex as it swirls around you.

The fourth ray is the white ray of purity, harmony, and hope. Archangel Gabriel and the purity ray of white light surrounds and soothes you, bringing harmony to your life. Allow any situations or issues into your mind that need harmony or hope to surround them. Welcome Archangel Gabriel into your life and accept her gifts as she infuses her energy into you, purifying your body and mind; igniting the candle of hope to burn within you. We thank Archangel Gabriel for sharing this wonderful gift with us as we breathe and find ourselves once more in the energy vortex.

The fifth colour that you become aware of is green, and the fifth ray is associated with Archangel Raphael and is the ray of healing and truth. Allow the healing energy of the green ray and Archangel Raphael to wash over and through you. This ray heals the Earth as well as all the beings that live on it and in it. Therefore as you sit in this healing energy allow the healing energy to heal yourself, but also send some to Mother Earth and all her children that live on her. As we accept this healing for ourselves we start to look inside ourselves for spiritual truth and truth in situations that we are in, and send healing energy and light to them. You breathe the green light in once more and find ourselves once more in the energy vortex.

The sixth colour that you become aware of is gold and this ray is concerned with peace. The energy of Archangel Uriel surrounds you and pours peace into your soul with his golden energy. The vibrations of peace and love surrounds you and pours into every aspect of your life including people you are connected to, situations you are in, and places where you live and work. Archangel Uriel gives you the gift of inner peace and places it into your heart, to call upon when next you need it. You breathe in this energy of Archangel Uriel and peace and once again find yourself in the energy vortex.

The seventh and final colour that the Archangels draw your attention to is the colour violet and this is the ray of Freedom, mercy, and transmutation. The Archangel associated with this ray is Archangel Zadkiel and as his warm and loving energy surrounds you, you become aware of the energy of transmutation that converts any energy into love and healing. This energy floods your body transmuting any negativity in your thoughts, body, and life. His mercy flows through you as your emotions are transmuted into loving energy. Finally the energy of freedom flows from this violet energy and Archangel Zadkiel into you, igniting the violet flame within you and liberating your soul to fly into your true spiritual self. You breathe in this energy again and as you do so you once again find yourself in the energy vortex of light.

As you stand in this energy vortex, you send thanks

to the Archangels who have worked with you, clearing blocks and introducing you to working with the seven rays of enlightenment. The white sparkling energy starts to fade around you and goes into Mother Earth to heal her, and you start to become aware once more of the room around you. You wiggle your fingers and toes to ensure your spiritual self used in this meditation is once again grounded in your physical body.

And now it's over to you................

I have tried to keep the outline of the techniques I use in my own life and keep them simple, as I believe that is how the Angels intend us to work with them – simply without confusion, regret, or complications.

Angels are the best friends and guides any of us can use. If there is a beautiful lake of life we are the pebbles that are thrown into it, our Angels are the closest ripples to us. They are with us every moment of every day, and when life feels like it is closing in around us, then you can be sure that your Guardian Angels are working overtime to send you signs, Earth Angels, and divine inspiration to guide you back into the light.

This book is the field guide to how I stay in touch with my best and closest friends (the Angels), to how I hear the divine guidance that they send me, and how you can now do the same. Always remember that Angels ask us to share, both our bodies and our souls with Mother Earth. Every animal and person is an extension of her and you never know when your Angel Within will call on you to be the next Earth Angel sent to touch the life of a person, so allow your presence to be gentle as even the slightest touch leaves a handprint on the hearts of those we meet.

Claire xx.

Claire can be contacted through Angelic Whispers at
www.angelicwhispers.co.uk.

Printed in Great Britain by
Amazon.co.uk, Ltd.,
Marston Gate.